Jim Clark
Portrait of a great driver

Jim Clark
Portrait of a great driver

Graham Gauld

in collaboration with
Ian Scott Watson
Graham Hill · Jackie Stewart
John Surtees · Gérard Crombac
Bill Bryce · Eoin Young
Walter Hayes · Colin Chapman

Foreword by Stirling Moss

ARCO PUBLISHING COMPANY, Inc. New York

Published 1968 in the United States by
ARCO PUBLISHING COMPANY, Inc.,
219 Park Avenue South, New York, N.Y. 10003

© The Hamlyn Publishing Group Limited, 1968

Reprinted 1969

Library of Congress Catalog Card Number 68-55305

ARCO Catalog Number 668-01842-9

Printed in Great Britain

Foreword
by Stirling Moss

Jimmy Clark was a humble man and a worthy World Champion. More than that, he was the best driver of his time. I qualify this statement with "his time", only because I do not think one can compare the Clarks, the Fangios and the Nuvolaris, any more than one can compare Roger Bannister with the current record miler. This does not mean that he was better or not as good, merely that a comparison is just not feasible.

Jimmy had great gifts, but he did not stop there, he made it his business to polish and shape them until he had no peer. When you watched him, you knew that a master was at work.

He will be missed by his friends, for his company; by his competitors, for the targets he set them; and by spectators, for his artistry.

S.M.
London, June, 1968

Contents

Acknowledgements

This book could not have been written using the recollections of one person only; thus in preparing it I spent some time with many people who knew Clark well. A tight editorial timetable was set, but I wanted to gather together the views of a lot of people who were close to Clark and to present them as a composite picture, not of a machine but of a man.

In addition to those who have contributed material for individual chapters, I would like to thank many other friends who have helped me in this difficult task. In particular I would like to thank Eric Dymock, a fellow Scot and motoring journalist; Jimmy's accountant and financial adviser, Chris Weir, who gave moral support when it was necessary; the journalists, motor sporting enthusiasts and friends, who added grains of information to fill in parts of this story, photographers, and finally David Hodges.

GRAHAM GAULD

List of Illustrations

The publishers are grateful to the organizations and individuals who have contributed illustrations to this book: Michael Cooper, Gerard Crombac, Philippe Dreux, Eric della Faille, The Ford Motor Company Ltd., Graham Gauld, David Hodges, the Editor of *Motor*, Jos. Reinhard, Michael Turner.

Introduction

It would have been all too easy to write a standard book about Jim Clark. After all, his achievements in motor racing have caused the record books to be re-written, and these statistical hard facts are freely available to those who make a study of this aspect of motor racing. In other words this book could have followed the time-honoured pattern, but when I was asked to write it I had mixed feelings.

Only two weeks had passed since Jimmy had been killed, the senses were still numbed, the reality that Jimmy wouldn't be around any more scarcely dawning. Indeed, had not a mutual journalist friend of Jimmy's and of mine, fellow Scot Eric Dymock, referred the publishers to me I might not have been writing these words.

Four years ago *Jim Clark At the Wheel* was published, a book which I helped Jimmy to write; his autobiography. It was written under pressure, yet when I look back on it it was a remarkably simple book to write for anyone who knew Clark well, knew that he could talk lucidly about motor racing and what it meant to him, and knowing that factually he had something of a photographic memory for minute details. On the other hand, faced as I was with writing a biography of Clark on my own without his assistance, I suddenly realised that no one person could write such a book.

In my mind Jim Clark meant many things to many people. I realized this most forcibly after his funeral, for it is obvious that many people from all walks of life felt they knew Jim Clark although they had never met him. Their motivations for liking Clark were often as varied. A middle-aged businessman told me he felt that Clark represented to him all that he would expect of his son. He represented the modern young man who conducted his public life well, who was worldly in his approach to life, and who epitomised the modern young Scot. Then there were the young people, the teenagers and pre-teenagers that I heard about: the seven-year old son of Claude Leguezec, the Team Manager of Matra, who used to go to bed in Jim Clark pyjamas; or the little Scots boy who, on the evening of Jim Clark's death, disappeared to his room, shut himself in and then removed his school diploma from its frame and replaced it with a photograph of Clark. The enthusiasts of this generation saw him as a Nuvolari, Fangio and Moss rolled into one. To those who are sentimental his loss was as hard to bear as the loss of a close friend. . . .

Therefore the compilation of this book had to be achieved by talking to a number of people about Clark— people he worked with, people he worked for and people he knew and liked. Clark in a way was an enigma, for he was content to sit back and allow you to form your own opinion about him without giving too many clues himself. He didn't like discussing himself too much but at the same time, when making a point that needed qualification, he wouldn't hesitate to inform you of the fact that *he* was World Champion, or that *he* had done this and that.

What I have sought to do in this book, therefore, is to show a little of the personality, the charm and the character of Jim Clark. In an age of cynicism, he was, with his friends, a very open and sincere person. This was not to say, however, that he was devoid of such natural human traits as anger, annoyance and pique, as some of his obituaries might have indicated.

In places this book is sentimental and of this I am not ashamed, for in his close friends Jimmy evoked a certain brand of sentimentality which was deeply sincere and it would be foolish to disguise feelings, honestly felt, for the sake of maintaining the ridiculous posture of the British stiff upper lip.

At the same time there are contradictions, for different people often had contrasting views about him and came to separate conclusions. I have not sought to rewrite these for I feel that in the end the reader should build up his own picture.

The preparations for the book held for me their own fascination. They took place during a week in early May which was hectic to the point of mirroring the kind of pace which Clark and his fellow racing drivers take as normal in their world-wide wanderings. I look back on the bleakness of Snetterton racing circuit at dusk after a shower, sitting in a Cortina talking to Graham Hill about Jimmy as a team mate, and to the sheer contrast of lounging in the flat of French motoring journalist Gerard Crombac in Montmartre two days later, while outside tourists clamoured around the paintings of the artist community which seemed to be congregated under Crombac's window.

As was the case with most people in the early days, I first met Jim Clark through Ian Scott Watson. While I honestly cannot remember how, in fact, we met, it must certainly have been at a Charterhall race meeting or on a rally. At that time I was the fledgling sports editor of Scotland's *Motor World* magazine with nose to grindstone, ear to ground. Being obviously willing to listen, I was naturally given the treatment on Jimmy by Ian. This was 1955 and the sum total of Clark's motor sporting experience was a few rallies with Berwick and District Motor Club. Through Scott Watson and Clark I met some of the other Border farmers who were rallying and as I had been competing at the time as navigator for a Perthshire farmer, Ron Dalglish, it was obvious that we had a lot in common. Indeed Scott Watson, the innovator, decided that we should form a team to compete in rallies and the club race meetings at Charterhall. It was felt that Ecurie Ecosse should not get all the limelight. The team was called Ecurie Agricole and Scott Watson, who was a bit of an amateur artist, sketched our own car sticker based on Enzo Ferrari's prancing horse badge; only ours incorporated a tractor rampant. We called ourselves "Ecurie Agricole—the team for the agriculture vultures". I was not a man of the soil and as I had been named team manager I had to do something to justify my existence. My final initiation was to mow Auchterarder's cricket pitch with a Ferguson tractor and three mowers. Having done this I was invested with an ear of corn and let into the club. It was all late teenage fun, particularly when we entered four cars at Charterhall one meeting and Ecurie Ecosse only had three. Mind you, their three cars were C-type Jaguars whilst our four were a DKW, a Sunbeam Talbot, and two Triumph TR2s—formidable opposition!

I will leave the direct comments on Jimmy's early career to Ian Scott Watson but will recall some of our trips together in those formative years. For instance, to the last meeting at the Crimond circuit in Aberdeenshire, when Jimmy took the D-type on a trailer, using Scott Watson's Thames 15 cwt. van as the tow car. While Scott Watson went on ahead in the Porsche, I travelled in the van. Trouble was the van was empty and, with the weight of the trailer, it was a job to keep on the road at any worthwhile speed. Whenever we got into one of the high speed snakes that are inevitable when towing a heavy trailer with a light vehicle, Clark would simply give the steering a wild jerk which would shake out the tail of the trailer and get it on an even keel again. I dread to think of the reactions of other people on that road that day! Once at Crimond Clark suggested I go round with him in the Porsche to find out whether he should race it on Michelin X tyres or the Dunlop racing tyres. He liked the Xs but liked even more the way he could slide the car on the racing tyres; my opinion was completely valueless as I was just waiting for him to stop. . . .

Actually, driving with Jimmy was often rather dull even though he did tend to press on. When preparing *Jim Clark At the Wheel* we drove down from Glasgow to his house in Duns in Colin Chapman's Ford Galaxie, with

Ian Scott Watson sound asleep along the back seat, and at around 3 a.m. we were on the long straight out of Dalkeith at about 125 m.p.h. with the radio playing. Clark had just finished saying how good the car was at this speed and how pleasant it was to listen to the late night music when all of a sudden he lost control. In a flash the car was wiggled straight again and he just laughed. Not so Scott Watson, who shot up on the back seat in alarm—"What was that?" "Oh, it was nothing Ian, get back to sleep" remarked Clark. "Look, that was ice back there" said Scott Watson, strangely wide awake now. "Havers" said Clark and carried on. About a mile further on we came up a slight hill and with his farmer's eyes Clark scanned the sky and observed that ". . . maybe it was ice, the sky is clear enough for it but we'll soon find out". With that he engaged a lower gear on the automatic box, kicked the accelerator and the car waltzed gently up the road sideways. It had been ice!

Flying with Clark was also an interesting experience. He applied the same degree of dedication to it as he did to his racing. I remember flying with him from Elstree to Edinburgh one afternoon when high winds had grounded most of the schedule airlines. We checked at the Met. office at Elstree and were told of 80 m.p.h. headwinds, so we were in for a long trip. I still had doubts about these small flying machines and these were in no way dispelled when Jimmy couldn't fire up one of the engines. He laughed and pointed out that he hadn't switched on the fuel pump; I curled deeper into my seat and wondered what else he had forgotten. The flight was uneventful save that the weather made Clark's job pretty tough.

Talking of private flying, Clark was of the opinion that the businessmen who, say, flew a long distance, did some work and then flew home, were stretching a point as modern flying, particularly in Britain, needs a great deal of concentration. By the time we reached Newcastle on that flight the clouds had cleared and it was dark below. As we had both rallied in Border country we spent the rest of the way to Edinburgh navigating by sight—a fascinating experience.

In recent years Jimmy had changed somewhat in his outward approach to life and, though he was a very genuine person, he had a dislike of being quizzed about his private life or his financial affairs. When cornered on this he would lapse into a monosyllabic interchange or indeed would quite openly be rude. I know of one young girl reporter on a National Scottish newspaper who faced a reluctant Clark on one occasion. After the interchange – with Clark piling on the brimstone – she returned to her older and more experienced Editor and complained that Jim Clark was the rudest person she had ever interviewed. Certainly, to an innocent bystander, some of Clark's interchanges with the Press were quite unpleasant and in utter contrast to his conversations with people who were more interested in his job.

As Clark often explained, he was mediocre at school and was not really a sports fan, though he did play hockey and cricket. Once, when I suggested that perhaps he was a sprinter, he replied by pointing out that in a race of five he usually finished fifth (nevertheless, in time we were to see him, in a motor racing role, outsprint even the fastest men in Le Mans starts). He was even then fascinated by motor racing it is true, and followed the sport in the pages of *Motor* and *Autosport* when at boarding school. He even admitted to buying an autographed photograph of Stirling Moss after seeing his first motor race, when visiting an Aunt who lived near Brands Hatch.

By the time Scott Watson's DKW drive came along Clark had competed in quite a few rallies and he was to win the Border Rally, which at that time, the mid-fifties, was a rough event similar to the special stage Internationals of today. The roads used were the old Roman ones which criss-crossed the Border and North of England country. His navigator on that occasion was Andrew Russell, another Border farmer, with whom he did a number of events in a Triumph TR3. I often tried to get him to go back to rallies, and in 1958 attempted to persuade him to use his influence to get a car for us to compete in the Tour de France rally, but this he resisted. I think part of the reason was that he hated to be driven. When in fact he did make a return to rallying in the 1966 R.A.C. Rally, he did so with the thoroughness which was so typical of him. Whereas most people thought that Jimmy was in that event for publicity, he was determined to have a real go at it.

When he left Scotland to live in London and started competing on the International scene I saw less of Jimmy but, whenever we did meet, he would give me all the information I might ask for. Indeed it was quite surprising just how much he valued friendships he made before he started racing. Shortly after his death I received a letter from a mutual friend, Neil Brown, who used to compete with a Triumph TR2 back in 1955. Now a stockbroker in

Los Angeles, Brown had been surprised on meeting Jim Clark eight years later at Riverside to find that Jimmy literally continued conversations they had had all that time ago just as though nothing had happened in between.

As a result of this loyalty, Jim Clark never lost any friends on his way to the top.

A Champion's Career
– Graham Gauld

The date was April 7, 1968, it was 2.40 in the afternoon and in Glasgow it was one of those weepy Spring days when you never know exactly what to do with yourself. The telephone rang and a friend on one of the newspapers blurted out his short message "Jim has had it; Jim Clark is dead."

The fact didn't quite register for a second but when it did it shot through me like a laser beam and I mumbled through the rest of the conversation. The memories came flooding back and then I thought of the argument I had had just two days before with a group of particularly cynical newspapermen on the very subject of racing and death and Jim Clark in particular. I selfishly thought of how all my arguments had perished in this one accident. After all he had never seen the colour of his own blood and now, in one fell swoop, he was gone.

In Hockenheim, Germany, another friend, the American journalist Jerrold Sloniger who also knew Clark, was penning for the U.S. Services magazine *Overseas Weekly* ". . . Somehow I can't believe it yet. I'll wake tomorrow, it will be race day and I'll wonder if Jim can work his magic with a sick automobile. None of the facts make sense, least of all the fact that one of the

world's most careful drivers, a master at leaving that
vital margin, simply crashed."

The race was not very important; although it was the
first event in the European Formula 2 Championship the
entry was not terribly brilliant. Hockenheim was new
to Clark and the indications were that he wasn't greatly
impressed with its somewhat featureless layout and fast
curves. The cars hadn't been running well and in practice
Clark had spun with a locking brake. In the race he was
lying eighth and trying his best with an engine that didn't
seem to be giving full power. Two kilometres out on the
fifth lap, when he was approaching a curve on full throttle,
the car went out of control and smashed into trees. Clark
was killed instantly. What happened in these last frac-
tions of a second really don't matter; they will not bring
Clark back to us. In my opinion, we should be allowed
to keep our own theories intact and not have them
'proved' or 'disproved.' To most of the people who knew
him and raced against him the theory of a driver error
is unthinkable, no matter what facts emerge, so surely we
each should be left with our own conclusions, if only we
maintain our own illusions?

In the beginning Jim Clark had no illusions, certainly no
illusions about ever becoming a racing driver. He has
admitted to reading motor sport magazines in his youth
when at school at Loretto, a public school just outside
Edinburgh. He had been sent there to round off his
education, but would never admit to being anything
better than average at school.

The Clarks were a farming family and Jimmy was born
in Kilmaddy in the ancient county of Fife. (In conversa-

tion Jackie Stewart's father once remarked that one of Jackie's grandparents had something to do with the Clark family in Fife and it would be interesting to consult the rolls in Edinburgh and find out whether, as was suggested, there might have been a family connection between the two of them.)

Later the family moved to Berwickshire and the rolling hills around Chirnside and Duns. The family consisted of James Clark senior, his wife, their four daughters and Jimmy. As soon as he left school, Jimmy was given one of the farms to run, Edington Mains, which boasted a solidly built farmhouse with walls some three feet thick in places. Edington Mains has about 1,250 acres of arable land and, whereas the impression was always given that he was a sheep farmer, the farm was mainly in crops. Clark also had some Irish cattle which were fattened up and sold each year and did breed some sheep (the family had three pedigree flocks, one of Border Leicesters, one of Suffolk Downs and one of Oxford Downs, the rams being sold at the local Kelso ram sales).

To make sure that Clark ate fairly regularly he had a loyal housekeeper in Helen McCormick, who always seemed to have tea brewing whenever one arrived. And there was Sweep the dog who investigated each visitor by walking round the car and performing a natural function on the hub caps. You were always made welcome at Edington Mains!

Inside—you normally entered from the back door in the yard—there was the dark yet cosy kitchen with one of those giant kitchen ranges found in farm houses everywhere. A door led into a short corridor with a small back lounge to the right, while another short corridor ran to the left with a small study in one direction and the front door entrance hall and stairway to the other.

Whenever I was there the little back lounge was the headquarters and it was noticeable that Clark's more prized trophies were kept there; a Michael Turner painting over the fireplace, the Indianapolis 'Rookie of the Year' plaque beside the door and the sentimental small trophies from the Border Motor Racing Club on the sideboard. Towards the end trophies overflowed into every room and I remember at one time when he was going through one of his anti-*Daily Express* periods he kept one of their trophies in the kitchen! Upstairs, eventually, he had a trophy room laid out and was very careful with visitors as by this time his collection had considerable value, including for example, the Esso Golden Helmet presented to him in recognition of his many victories under the Esso banner.

Back in the small lounge you collapsed into a chunky settee and Clark would flop into one of the armchairs. Afternoon tea was properly served on a trolley with a pretty patterned tea service and there were always plenty of home-baked scones.

Everything was unpretentious and the only concession to modernity about the small lounge was the fireplace which had been bought on the spur of the moment by Clark and Ian Scott Watson, who simply chose the first fireplace they saw. One realised that Clark was a bit disorganised in many ways . . .

One winter's afternoon when I was down there Clark explained that we had to listen for an aircraft around

4.0 p.m. as Colin Chapman, his wife and Jimmy's girl friend Sally Stokes were due to arrive. Chapman had never flown to the farm before and I remember raising an eyebrow when Clark explained how he had told Colin to find the farm. " I told him to fly to Berwick-on-Tweed and then along the line of the River Tweed from the mouth at Berwick. When he saw the first red barns on the north side he was to circle the house until he saw signs of life." At 4.0 p.m. we went outside and scanned the skies but there was no sign of action. At 4.20 p.m. there was the distant sound of an aircraft and we gazed at the slowly darkening skies and finally saw it, a speck in the distance flying in the wrong direction. Immediately Clark scrambled into a Ford Galaxie—Chapman's car, actually — and we shot down the narrow farm road, through the esses near the main road junction and turned for Berwick. We had just set off and had reached about 70 m.p.h. when the 'plane suddenly turned and flew towards us. Clark flashed the headlights and Chapman dipped the wings in acknowledgement. A hand brake turn and we were zooming back past the farm and up a side road to the edge of a field filled with sheep. Clark whistled on his dog, jumped the five bar gate and lit out after the sheep with the dog at his heels. Between them they rounded the sheep up and sent them off to the far side of the field whilst Chapman made a couple of passes. On the third he almost touched down then flew off. "He's gone to Winfield", said Clark. So it was back into the Galaxie for another dash across country to the disused airfield, sometime circuit where Clark had run in some sprints in the earliest days of his motor sport career. There we picked up Chapman and his passengers.

In general layout the farm had changed little over the years and it had a family ghost. This was the Grey Lady who Jimmy claimed to have seen when he was very young and taken for his mother. But, on the following morning his mother said she hadn't been near his room. Since then a number of people have been visited by the ghost. Once, when Jimmy and I were preparing some notes for his autobiography, we had a wild session with Jackie Stewart and Paddy Hopkirk. As we talked into the small hours it was decided that Stewart and I would share one room, while Paddy slept in another. Jackie and I thought it was all very funny because we believed that Jimmy had put Paddy into the haunted room but in fact we were told in the morning that we had been sleeping in it . . .

Back at the beginning of his career, Clark dabbled in motor sport at a club level with a few rallies and the odd sprint. His father had allowed him to buy a Sunbeam Talbot Mark III saloon which he used to terrorise half of Berwickshire and in it he did some improbable things in various events. Away from motor sport it was also reputed to have vaulted a hedge into a field after a particularly hectic Young Farmers Club social!

At that time the farm was work and motor sport was play. He had met Ian Scott Watson, who was to play a major role in his development as a racing driver, and in 1955 he competed in his first International motor sporting event as navigator to his farming neighbour Billy Potts in an Austin Healey 100. For the record they finished thirteenth in the big sports car class – none too brilliant. A year later, almost to the month, he had his first race at Crimond in Aberdeenshire and was blooded; from then on it was only a matter of time.

Ian Scott Watson was Clark's great champion. Scott Watson pushed and persuaded Clark to give racing a try, and in time Clark began to realise that he enjoyed racing, but he had neither the ambition nor the strength of character to push himself forward.

Meanwhile the reports in the Scottish motor papers told the story. As sports editor of *Motor World*, the Scottish weekly magazine, I was at most of the events, such as the M.G. Car Club (Scottish Centre) sprint at an old disused army camp at Stobs near Hawick. This was a twisting little course and Clark had entered his Sunbeam as usual, whilst Scott Watson was running his black DKW. After the practice session the Stewards held a meeting and the subject raised was this driver J. Clark in the Sunbeam. Scrutineer Archie Craig, now Chairman of Scottish Motor Racing Club, recalled that the Stewards had been called together to see whether some censure should be given to Clark, for they felt sure that if he ran in the event he would have the world's biggest accident. After talking it out it was decided not to act but to wait and see. In the event proper Clark was impressive and I wrote at the time: ". . . His driving was at times heartstopping, the car clearing the ground completely on the downhill stretch, and his times in the saloon car classes were only beaten by Hughes' Porsche." A day later he saw off everyone else in the Berwick and District Motor Club gymkhana, and so it went on. Four class wins in the Berwick sprint at

Winfield in Sunbeam and DKW, a broken radiator in the Border Rally, and then that October day at Charterhall when he won the Border Motor Racing Club Trophy in Scott Watson's Porsche 1600 Super, the event which set his future course, even though he did not realize this at the time.

Border Reivers, a Scottish racing team run by Jock McBain (who had raced a Cooper 500 in the early days of that racing class,) then bought a D-type Jaguar for Clark to drive. He tried it once on the bumpy straight at Charterhall and then packed it up to go to his first race meeting at Full Sutton near York. This circuit had a short but historic life. Prepared at great expense as an air force base by the Americans, it was abandoned within a year. The circuit was beautifully paved and at the first meeting Clark won almost everything there was to win, becoming the first man to lap the circuit at over 100 m.p.h. Later that season Full Sutton was taken into commission again and as a racing circuit has never been heard of since. But in its short life span as a circuit Jim Clark was its master.

A trip to Spa shortly afterwards for a sports car race gave Clark his first taste of real fear. I think this experience, literally only his second race in a proper sports-racing car, was etched so deeply into his mind that he never liked Spa and never liked fast circuits with fast open corners and trees. It is sad to think that, almost exactly ten years to the week after this, Clark was killed on a similar type of circuit with fast open corners bordered by trees. On that day in 1958, however, he was too busy keeping his emotions in check to worry about the future.

His hero, Masten Gregory, won the race in an Ecurie Ecosse Lister-Jaguar but Archie Scott Brown, another Scot, crashed and was killed. It had been wet and Clark recalled noticing that the corner where this accident happened was wetter than the rest; he therefore treated it with care. In another coincidence of fate Clark's Lotus team mate Alan Stacey was also killed at Spa in his second Grand Prix race. Jimmy never overcame his forebodings about the circuit; after winning the Belgian Grand Prix for the fourth time running he bemoaned the fact that he had never won at Monaco, a circuit he loved, but had won at Spa four times, on a circuit he hated.

In that season of 1958 he crammed in many events, not only with the D-type Jaguar but with Scott Watson's Porsche and his own white Triumph TR3, which had been the 1957 Motor Show car. Back at the local Stobs sprint he took first and second places, with the Porsche and the Triumph (taking second overall when the Porsche was matched against sports-racing cars). At Crimond, in the last meeting ever held at the Aberdeenshire circuit, he won the sports car race with the D-type and finished a creditable fourth in the small sports car race in the Porsche. This was a nostalgic meeting for Clark, because two years earlier at the same meeting he had started on his racing career.

The real sting in 1958 came at the tail of the year. At his local circuit, Charterhall, he came up against Ecurie Ecosse with Ron Flockhart in a D-type Jaguar and Innes Ireland in a Lister-Jaguar. This battle was one of many with Flockhart and it didn't help matters, when in a game of outbraking at the end of the long straight, Ireland spun off on to the grass. On this occasion Ecurie Ecosse triumphed in both races they entered.

For 1959 Border Reivers had planned to buy a single-seater Formula 2 Lotus for Clark but, after trying one out and later watching Graham Hill lose a wheel in the same car, Clark decided that Lotus cars were not safe and certainly not for him; he would stick to big hairy sports cars. At the Lotus test, however, Scott Watson had ordered a pre-production Lotus Elite and they were due to collect it in time for the Boxing Day Brands Hatch meeting that year. After much phoning Scott Watson and Clark caught the Edinburgh-London train at Berwick and picked up their car. At the circuit, Scott Watson overheard Colin Chapman and Mike Costin – who were also down to drive Elites – trying to sort out which one of them would win the race, for apparently their wives had both insisted that this be their last motor race. Scott Watson was incensed at this and, hearing a trackside bookmaker offer 10-1 odds on Clark to win the race, lavishly placed 5s. on his hero. As it turned out Clark gave Chapman the toughest race of his life and led him until a slower car which they were lapping spun and hit Clark's car hard enough to let Chapman through to take the lead and win. Scott Watson never placed another bet in motor racing.

The Lister-Jaguar bought by Border Reivers was not one of the boat-shaped Mike Costin-designed cars but a one-off which had been driven in the T.T. by Archie Scott Brown and later by Bruce Halford (who ran in Formula I races at the time with a Maserati 250 FI). Clark had been impressed when watching the car in action with Halford at the wheel but when he took it over to drive it back to Scotland he found he could hardly get into it and ended up driving home in his stockinged feet. The mechanics at McBains hacked a piece out of the bodywork to get the seat further back and he embarked on his 1959 season with the Lister. This was a fairly reliable car – albeit with no brakes – and he had some good races and places. His drive in the wet at Aintree against top opposition was hailed as masterly but even at this time he didn't take his racing seriously and indeed suffered various guilt complexes about racing at all. Had it not been for Scott Watson's prodding we would never have seen or heard of Clark again, but he kept on going under the Scott Watson pressure. It is interesting when looking at his progress later, when he became extremely self-assured, to recall, that, during this early period, he appeared to have an almost masochistic desire to be goaded into carrying on with his racing.

With the Elite, too, he did well and the Border Reivers secured an entry at Le Mans. However, there was some confusion at Lotus, so the car wasn't prepared and there was some talk of Lotus taking over the entry. Eventually a compromise was arranged, so Clark drove the car as a Lotus entry with the pit work carried out by Border Reivers. His co-driver was chosen by Chapman and turned out to be a cheery fair-haired individual called John Whitmore, who became one of Jimmy's first friends outside his Scottish racing circles. In the race the car suffered mechanical trouble, yet finished tenth and a second in its class.

After the race Scott Watson was impressed with the car and arranged with Colin Chapman to buy it, and

Hockenheim, April 7th, 1968

Early days. Cooling down in the Border Reivers D-type after a victory at Charterhall (*above*), and throwing Scott Watson's Goggomobil around in a driving test during the 1957 "Suez" petrol crisis (*below*)

Another driving test, in the Sunbeam Talbot 90 which was an early maid of all work (*above*). First race in a rear-engined car, in the Porsche 1600S at Charterhall in 1957 (*below*)

Concentration.   Cornering the Triumph TR3 in a
Rest-and-be-Thankful hill-climb in 1958

Clark raced it in Britain the rest of that year. He naturally continued to compete in the various Scottish events, setting a new sports car record at Bo'ness Hill Climb in June. Back on the Continent for the *Autosport* 'World Cup' race for small GT cars the Elite seized its back axle and Clark was left on the sidelines to blaze inwardly, for the sheer competitiveness of racing was beginning to seep into his bones and one sensed that before very long he must realise that a career lay ahead in full-time motor racing. Unknown to Clark at this time Jock McBain, the guiding light of Border Reivers, was already thinking in terms of a single-seater ride but it was to be some time before a serious opportunity arose.

In August Clark had his one and only race for Ecurie Ecosse, in the T.T. at Goodwood, driving a Tojeiro-Jaguar. At this time the Scottish team, with Le Mans wins in 1956 and 1957 tucked under their belt, were sticking to British sports racing cars, although the pickings were beginning to thin out. Indeed, David Murray was to admit later that during this period their Le Mans wins had gone to their heads and possibly their judgement was in error as to the cars they were using. This was quite understandable, for this relatively small Scottish team, with only a fraction of the backing that went with most other private teams in motor racing, had with these two Le Mans wins helped Jaguar's fortunes when the factory team was in the doldrums. Now they had a D-type and the Tojeiro-Jaguar, cars which were beginning to lose their competitive edge against more modern equipment.

At the Tourist Trophy Jimmy was to be further amazed at his own ability. It seems strange that, even at this stage in the game, Clark should still be naive about his driving — he approached the Goodwood race with a certain amount of trepidation. Masten Gregory was, in his opinion, the top sports car driver and here he was sharing a car with him. Other people in the race had their own problems because, as the final event in the World Sports Car Championship, there promised a Donnybrook between the respective teams of Porsche, Aston Martin and Ferrari ; the intrusion of a lone Ecurie Ecosse Tojeiro counted for little in the overall race picture. To Clark it meant a lot.

In the race the battle up front was hot and furious and there was drama when Moss came into the pits with the leading 3-litre Aston Martin DBR1. When it was jacked up and being refuelled petrol leaked onto the hot exhaust and instantly the car was blazing furiously. The fire spread to the wooden pit counter and by the time it was under control the Aston Martin pits were a shambles and the car a burned-out wreck. Clark saw all this happening, little knowing that within six months he would be driving that same Aston Martin in races, for this was the car Border Reivers bought for the 1960 season.

Aston Martin had their problems but Clark had few, for in the race he found himself lapping Goodwood as quickly as Gregory. Suddenly he began to enjoy life. On his second stint in the car he was taking the chicane in two big opposite lock slides and was running a comfortable seventh overall. Then Masten Gregory took over again, only to stuff the car into the bank at Woodcote in the biggest possible way and write it off. Masten himself stood up on the seat and was catapulted over the crowd to escape with a broken collar bone and a shaking. (For David Murray this was almost the last straw for he had seen the same sort of thing happen to his cars before.) So the race ended with Aston Martin winning the Championship, Clark suddenly filled with confidence and Masten Gregory looking for another ride. Clark never again drove for Ecurie Ecosse for their paths never crossed. Meanwhile, as the season came to an end and after considering a Porsche for Clark, Border Reivers negotiated for their Aston Martin.

For Clark this was a time to sit back and take stock. He knew that his family were openly hostile to his racing but he was more and more enthusiastic about it. Yet he was very conscious of the fact that he should have more experience before moving any farther up the ladder. He had earlier eschewed single-seaters for big sports cars but he began to realise that, if he wanted to go very far in racing, he had to get into single-seater racing cars – advice he was to pass on to Jackie Stewart when he too came to a moment of decision

At this point, and with everything going well for him, in stepped the late Reg Parnell, team manager for Aston Martin. Behind this scene was surely Jock McBain, the ebullient patron of Border Reivers, who knew Reg of old. Like Ian Scott Watson before him, McBain had faith in Clark's ability and he added weight to Scott Watson's already convincing arguments that Clark should stay in racing. When he eventually did become World Champion, Clark's greatest regret was that McBain hadn't lived to see this triumphal moment. Through McBain, then, Parnell contacted Jim Clark and talked positively about a

Formula I drive with Aston Martin in 1960. This was dismissed by Clark in his usual manner, although in fact he secretly wanted to try a Formula I car. Eventually a tentative date was set for a trial at Goodwood. Before then, however, there was the Boxing Day Brands Hatch meeting of 1959 where Clark drove a single-seater racing car for the first time.

During his races with the Elite he had become friendly with Graham Warner of the Chequered Flag, who was about to enter Formula Junior racing, a class which had been developed from an Italian suggestion for low cost racing, and which had received the blessing of the F.I.A. Already Elva were in the field with a high-tailed single-seater and there were other early cars using a variety of engines. But although others were first in the field, the big guns of Cooper and Lotus were to come along and dominate its early years. For the Boxing Day meeting at Brands Hatch, however, Clark had accepted a drive offered by Warner in a Junior car of his own construction, the Gemini. This was a conventional cigar-shaped front-engined racing car which George Hulbert of Speedwell had been working on. Unlike his later cars, which were tailored for his short body and wide shoulders, the Gemini was made to standard dimensions and Clark was cramped in the cockpit with little room for forearm movement. Coupled with this it was raining and the battery was flat, so his first single-seater ride was one he tended to forget about – later he didn't like to be reminded of it at all.

Beside him on the Brands Hatch grid, however, was a car which was to loom large in his future life. This was the prototype Lotus 18 Formula Junior car, and it was rear-engined. There had not been time to paint the car and the race was to show that Chapman's suspension settings were hopeless, but the writing was on the wall; Chapman had put the engine behind the driver and his layout was interesting. Neither Clark with his Gemini nor Chapman with his new Lotus, which was driven by Alan Stacey, achieved much success at the meeting. For Clark the Gemini and Formula Junior didn't seem attractive, for Chapman it was the well-worn path back to the drawing board. But the meeting wasn't without its drama, for in the GT race Clark was battling with Graham Warner in the Elites when he lost control at notorious Paddock Bend and bent a hub, putting himself out of the race. There was nothing really significant in this save that it was his first accident in a race, and when talking it over with me he admitted that he hadn't the faintest idea what had caused it. Eventually he concluded that he had given up trying to win the race and had relaxed his concentration. One wonders if a similar combination of circumstances could possibly have led to a lapse at Hockenheim, but it does seem unlikely in the extreme.

A new season approached and Clark was offered his trial at Goodwood for Aston Martin. By a strange coincidence Mike Costin of Lotus arrived with a Formula Junior Lotus and asked Clark to try it. This coincidence always struck me as being too good to be true, particularly as Clark drove in the Lotus Formula Junior team that season. It was February and it was cold. Patches of ice were hanging about on the circuit to catch the unwary and Clark did a few exploratory laps in a 4.2-litre Aston Martin DBR2. This was a good car and he liked the feel of it, possibly because—one always had this impression—he was more at ease in a car which was too powerful than in one which perhaps didn't have enough power. He had the knack of being able to control power and take it in his stride. There was never the feeling that he consciously developed from one stage to the next; his ability seemed constant and just needed to be sharpened with new sensations. Certainly, when he jumped from the sports car into the 2·5-litre Formula I car, he took to it like a duck to water. For him the car felt right, ran right and was powerful (although, in fact, this particular Aston Martin was not the most powerful car in Grand Prix racing and it was destined never to be successful; Aston Martin later withdrew from single-seater racing altogether).

So the courtship with Aston Martin continued into a second test session, and again Costin arrived at Goodwood with the Formula Junior Lotus. After getting Parnell's agreement, Clark tried the Junior immediately after a run in the Formula I Aston. The change he found remarkable for, from a reasonably conventional Formula I car, he jumped into the very latest in racing car design, the Lotus 18.

This proved to be a revelation, the car was ridiculously fast through the corners and, possibly for the first time, Clark began to realise just what handling meant. Up to then, in his big hairy sports cars, he had been used to brute power and lots of opposite lock; now he had a car which could be set up for a corner in the knowledge that it would go through on the quickest possible line without a waver and the driver thus had time to concentrate on driving technique.

Chapman had wanted to sign Clark for all forms of racing but the Aston Martin intervention saw him sign for Aston in Formula I and Lotus in Formula 2 and Formula Junior. To have signed Clark on a Formula I contract might well have been embarrassing, for in 1960 Chapman had plenty of drivers. He had Innes Ireland as team leader and had approached John Surtees, while Trevor Taylor was signed for Formula Junior and Alan Stacey in another Formula I car. It would have been just impossible for Clark to have come in as a contracted Formula I driver with all these other drivers – although it would have been interesting to see what would have happened had he done so!

It transpired that Clark had backed the wrong Grand Prix horse and he twiddled his thumbs waiting for his Aston Martin Formula I drive which never materialised, for the team retired from racing before the Dutch Grand Prix. Meanwhile, Clark had a Formula Junior car to drive and he found himself competing against John Surtees in the Ken Tyrrell Cooper Junior. They had some grand scraps at the beginning of that season.

'Back home' the Border Reivers had sold the Lister-Jaguar to an English club driver and invested in an Aston Martin DBR1 3000. This car's third place at Le Mans with Clark and Salvadori was its best showing, but with Clark's other commitments and the death of Jock McBain, it was never utilised fully in the seasons which followed and finally it was sold out of McBain's estate.

The first Lotus season started well with a win at Goodwood over John Surtees, and 1960 also saw Clark entering on the kind of life which he was to lead until his death.

One week he would be driving for Lotus in Belgium, the next for Border Reivers in Germany and so on. He was pretty wet behind the ears when going abroad and he even found talking to girls an embarrassment. In time this was to change, as was his attitude to life and racing generally.

Clark was very much the new boy in the team and he ran strictly to orders in the Formula 2 Brussels Grand Prix, but when with the Reivers he could run his own race. The Nürburgring fascinated him as it was a difficult circuit and very much a driver's circuit. At the Le Mans start of the 1000 km race he outsprinted Moss, which gave him a little bit of satisfaction, but Moss soon passed him and he had to be content with second place at the end of the first lap. This was too good to last, however, for the engine soon succumbed to valve trouble.

It was an exciting season full of new faces and places, when his first visit in Monaco brought him the same thrill of anticipation as Nürburgring had provided. He drove a Formula Junior Lotus, amazing himself, and even more the spectators, by taking nearly 10 seconds off the previous Junior lap record. When someone told him he had lapped faster than Fangio had done only three years previously with a Formula I car yet another brick was added to the wall of confidence he was building up within himself. But in the race he finished seventh after a high tension lead had come off and so began his trail of bad luck at Monaco, a circuit where he always wanted to win.

By this time he was beginning to have doubts about the Aston Martin deal. They had not produced a car for him at Monaco and at Zandvoort there were problems about starting, and Aston Martin withdrew. But at the same time Colin Chapman occasionally had a spare Formula I Lotus as John Surtees was still on a motor cycle contract, and one of his races clashed with the Dutch Grand Prix. Everything was cleared up and so, in June 1960, Jim Clark had his first Grand Prix drive for Lotus, for whom he was to drive eight consecutive seasons in the Formula I team. The race was uneventful— Clark worked his way up to fifth place before the gearbox seized, while Innes Ireland finished second. At Spa the following week Surtees was again missing and Clark took his place with Stacey and Ireland. This race, however, was not routine and, as when Clark had last raced at Spa, a driver was killed. This time it was Alan Stacey, his team mate, who was hit by a bird and killed instantly. In addition, Stirling Moss had crashed when a rear hub of his Lotus 18 collapsed, and Moss's protege Chris Bristow was killed. Michael Taylor in another Lotus had a steering failure. All in all, it was a tragic weekend for motor sport and for the young Team Lotus driver it was one to forget. It is hard to know what passed through his mind and if he had been true to his former pattern we could well have seen Clark retire from motor sport. But the signs were that his own philosophy of racing was beginning to emerge and his basic faith in himself was strengthening. One cannot stress too much the insecurity which Clark felt in the beginning and, whereas I feel that most racing drivers are motivated by something of an inferiority complex, I believe that Clark reached a stage where he had something of a superiority complex, which was controlled to the extent that he never let it show.

The Belgian race ended with Clark in fifth place, a brilliant effort in only his second Grand Prix yet one which to Clark meant little for he was too immersed in his own thoughts. Luckily Le Mans came along and the bustle which surrounds this event took his mind off the tragedies at Spa. In this event he ran the Reiver's Aston Martin with Roy Salvadori and they finished third overall, the highest placed British team, mainly due to Clark's brilliant driving in the wet and in a sickly car.

At the French Grand Prix his patriotic streak was given a fillip when Chapman signed Ron Flockhart to join Ireland and Clark to make up the only team of Scotsmen in Grand Prix racing up to then or since. Again Clark finished fifth, and by now his performances were being watched. He began to get offers of cars, such as Stirling Moss's new Lotus 19 for the sports car race before the British Grand Prix at Silverstone (a deal which fell through as the Grand Prix drivers were not allowed to compete in the supporting events).

The 1960 motor racing season was now in full swing and Clark had forgotten about the early nail biting period of waiting for the Aston Martin to turn up. He was getting into the feel of things, he was realising his limitations and he was getting to grips with the physical task of keeping up the pace of the International racing driver. His weight, which was formerly 11 stone 7 lb., dropped to 10 stone 8 lb. as his racing career speeded up and also he became fitter, not because he did exercises like Jackie Stewart, but simply because the constant physical effort of driving kept him superbly fit. His height tended to mask his tremendous strength. Indeed many people were surprised by the fact that he was so small, but he had broad shoulders and powerful forearms and a great deal of stamina. He needed it, for race followed race in quick succession and, whether he liked it or not, his destiny was to be motor racing.

He finished last in the British Grand Prix after being in third place and calling into the pits, then he retired with transmission trouble in the Guards Trophy at Brands Hatch, so the brightest moment of the season came in August when he finished third in the Portuguese Grand Prix driving a car which he had bent in practice and which had been cobbled up for the race in order to secure starting money. In Formula Junior he and his team mate Trevor Taylor were sweeping the boards and more and more often the results read Lotus, Lotus, Lotus. Towards the end of the season he had a nasty accident at Oulton Park when he touched wheels with Brian Naylor and he had another accident with John Surtees in the U.S. Grand Prix. Both of these hurt his pride more than his person.

He deliberated and signed for a further season with Lotus. This took him first on a winter trip around New Zealand, a country which obviously impressed him for afterwards he frequently spoke of it, and tried to get over there as often as he could. Something of the country reminded him of home and, though the farm was by this time being run for him, he was still sufficiently attached to it to return whenever he had free time.

The 1961 season was hardly successful, but it was one in which Clark developed his craft. The Formula I Lotus 18 gave way to the Lotus 21, which had potential but it didn't show its real worth until the last race of the year at Kyalami, in South Africa when Clark won the Rand Grand Prix. He followed this up with wins in the Natal Grand Prix and the South African Grand Prix, a non-Championship event that year. These three races and the Pau Grand Prix were the only events he won in 1961.

An event which remained in Clark's memory in 1961 was yet another tragedy, one in which he was directly involved. The repercussions were great and months were to pass before his mind could be at rest.

The scene was the Italian Grand Prix at Monza. The championship was bound to go to a Ferrari driver, with the young German Wolfgang von Trips being the most likely winner. Phil Hill, the American driver, was close – both of them had had a good season because Ferrari were so well prepared for the change of Formula that year. The Monza event, then, was one of these annual show races before the partisan crowd. They came along to see the Ferraris beat the opposition and this in fact happened. But there was tragedy too. Clark had a good start but, as expected, the Ferraris took command in the early laps. Von Trips for some reason had been delayed in the opening moments and he came rushing through the field, passing Clark and setting out after his Ferrari team mates. Down the back straight, however, Clark got in behind him and was towed along by the faster car. At the crucial moment he broke the slipstream and moved out to pass Von Trips, but the German driver had obviously not noticed that the Lotus was still close behind and he drove right into its path. The drivers were unable to avoid one another and cannoned onto the grass at high speed. Clark's car spun to a halt and he was unhurt but von Trips car vaulted over the banking and killed several spectators as well as the driver. The heart went out of the race; Phil Hill became Champion of the World but all around there was sadness – and Clark had the job of mentally talking himself back into racing once again.

He still had the Reivers Aston Martin but it was no longer eligible for the Tourist Trophy so he drove an Aston Martin DB4 GT in that race and also in the Paris 1000 km race at Montlhéry.

The final South African race was in Cape Town in January I and Clark finished second to Trevor Taylor. It had been a successful winter trip but back home all was not well. Innes Ireland had given Team Lotus their first Grand Prix win but his contract was not renewed for 1962. Out of this fact developed a bitter rivalry, which at times appeared nasty, between Ireland and Clark. The true facts behind this never came right out into the open but we can assume that it was patched up in time for, in his obituary to Clark, Ireland, as sports editor of *Autocar*, wrote a most moving piece of motoring journalism, which perhaps showed that the dispute was only an extension of the nervous energy both drivers put into their racing.

In February Clark went to Daytona Speedway in Florida on one of those odd driving missions he often undertook. This was to drive a Lotus Elite in the 1300 cc class of the Inter-Continental GT race. The battery failed when Clark was leading the race and he ended up fourth.

For Jimmy, American and Daytona was only just beginning to sink in. On his first visit to the States in 1960 he had been wide eyed and bushy tailed. He visited Hollywood and had been impressed by the scenery. One moving portion of the scenery was the amply constructed June Wilkinson who featured in a number of *Playboy* uncoverings. She had been persuaded to ride round the Riverside circuit with Innes in a Lotus – an operation to make the mind boggle. Innes, I believe, was afterwards speechless and Clark was obviously impressed by it all.

Clark had been taken to Daytona to have a look at the famous circuit, the home of Southern stock car racing. American stock car racing is related in some ways to European saloon car racing, but only American cars are used. It attracts a motley collection of drivers with real hair on their chests and, when offered a ride round the circuit with Fireball Roberts, then at the height of his career, Clark accepted and went with him in a Pontiac Bonneville. To Clark this was crazy motor racing, slip-streaming a tri-oval circuit with lap speeds of 150 m.p.h. He admitted to being terrified – not implausable as Clark was the world's worst passenger in any car, in any circumstances with any driver! Indeed I can only think of one occasion in which I drove him, and then he was kind enough not to comment but just smile wanly every so often.

To Clark, America brought home the realisation that European-style motor racing wasn't the only form of racing in the world. He was fascinated by things like

Destruction Derbies where he could ". . . see Chevvys, Fords, Buicks and Pontiacs driven by these brave men demolished before your eyes in the wildest, most dangerous event ever run on any speedway . . . all seats 2 dollars, children 50 cents." He felt that the Americans didn't need Europeans – a view which was shared by a number of American drivers as was made plain when Clark went over there after the big prize, Indianapolis.

The 1962 motor racing season promised well. It was the second year of the 1·5-litre Formula and, after a poor season in 1961, the Lotus-Climaxes began to get in the money. He won two of the opening events, the Lombank Trophy at Snetterton and the Aintree 200, so was well prepared for the first Championship Grand Prix, the Dutch at Zandvoort. This was one of the circuits he liked best and he led the race until the gearbox failed so he was classified ninth and gained no championship points. A week later, however, he drove one of his finest-ever races at the Nürburgring in the 1000 km race. The car was Chapman's latest brain child, the Lotus 23 rear-engined sports car. The chassis design was based on that of the single-seaters, it was rear-engined and sat low on the track. At Nürburgring, where handling really counts, Clark overwhelmed all the big cars and led the race in this tiny little bug of a car. The lead was short lived, however, as the exhaust manifold started to pour out fumes and he missed a gear and crashed.

A week later in the Monaco Grand Prix a good second place was lost to him when the engine failed—it was beginning to look like 1961 all over again. But then the dice began to fall in his favour and there began a tremendous cat and mouse battle with Graham Hill for the World Championship. After only two seasons in Grand Prix racing, Clark had arrived and in the Belgian Grand Prix he drove the monocoque Lotus 25 to a well-deserved victory, his first Grand Prix win. Between June 1962 and January 1968 he was to win another 24, and thus beat Fangio's Grand Prix record. He won again at Aintree and finished a magnificent fourth in the German Grand Prix after stalling on the starting line; he had forgotten to switch on his fuel pumps! He was well placed in the Championship and, when he won the U.S. Grand Prix, he was faced with a decider in the South African Grand Prix at East London on December 29.

This was to be a fateful race. Remember, in just one season Lotus and B.R.M. had got the edge on the Ferraris which had dominated in 1961, and now the World Championship was between the Lotus Climax and the B.R.M. On the face of it, Graham Hill was in a better position, for Clark had to make it an outright win. The strain of being in this position was beginning to tell and, whereas before he hadn't really given the Championship much thought, he was faced with the pressures from outside.

In the race he started well and kept Hill at bay. He even pulled out a good lead but then saw ominous signs of blue smoke indicating an oil leak somewhere. He dashed into the pits, letting Hill take the lead and it was found that a little metal plug had come loose . . . So Clark retired and Hill became World Champion in 1962.

The year had been successful, one which marked yet another landmark as he now realised, even if he hadn't

been willing to realise it before, that the World Championship was within his grasp.

Anyone who knew Clark well could tell you that this
was all he needed to make him resolve to win the World
Championship. Prior to this race I honestly don't think he
gave it a thought, but that stubborn streak in him came
out and he determined to have a real go in 1963.

Something else was on his mind too: Indianapolis.
Since Jack Brabham had raced in the '500' in 1961 others,
lured by the prize money and the prestige, had become
interested. Very quietly Lotus took the Watkins Glen
Grand Prix car to Indianapolis and, without having it
set up specially for the track, Clark managed to lap at
around 140 m.p.h. – this shook a few Americans. Though
few people knew about the future pattern of events, Dan
Gurney had previously talked with Chapman about the
possibility of using a modified V-8 Fairlane engine in a
Lotus Grand Prix car and letting it loose at Indy. The
outing with the 1·5-litre car after the Grand Prix was
intended simply to try out the handling. The results were
promising and they realised that the key to winning
Indianapolis was not to build a bigger catapult to push
you along the straights but to build-in roadholding to
take you round the corners faster. The big Indy roadsters
with their four-cylinder Offenhauser engines had live
axles and handled like pigs. The little Lotus was low on
the ground and had independent suspension; even without
offset suspension – standard practice on the regular
Indianapolis cars – the car was impressively fast.

What happened next made history, although Clark
had his own misgivings about it all. He often said that he

wished he had never been brought into the Indy project but I had the feeling that these statements carried less conviction than most of his others. For him it was a new challenge and when the Speedway officials put him through the driver's test at various speeds they little knew they were convincing him more and more that he had to go out and show everyone what he could do. The atmosphere was hostile in some respects, in others it was patronising. Clark was impressed by the organisation and by the sheer magnitude of the operation. He was amazed that by beating the big drum the promoters could get upwards of 250,000 spectators to pay just to watch the qualifying periods let alone the race.

The Lotus Indianapolis project was put into motion, with support from Ford U.S.A., and Clark prepared for the next Grand Prix season.

He had plenty of work to do. By now he was assisting in the development of a number of projects including the Lotus Cortina. Some time before he had driven a Ford Anglia with a Cosworth twin-cam engine and the combination had impressed him. Now he was doing the advance testing of the Lotus Cortina which was to be raced later that season. He found this car great fun and in the ensuing seasons he was to be seen racing it all over the world. To him it was fun and it gave the crowd something to enjoy. (It was not his first modern saloon car in racing, however, for he had tried a big Ford Galaxie at Brands Hatch once, but he didn't enjoy this car too much as he kept falling out of the seat!)

The 1963 season became hectic, with driving tests plus practice sessions at Indianapolis added to a full

Grand Prix season in Europe. Clark became a much-travelled man yet he could still find humour in odd moments – when, for example, after a meeting where 'plane connections were tight, Chapman's aircraft got bogged down in a muddy field trying to take off with Jimmy and Dan Gurney aboard. Finally they pushed the plane out of the mud and took off to catch their connection.

In 1963 the Lotus Formula I cars had fuel-injection Climax engines giving more power. At Monaco, Clark's nemesis, the fuel overflow pipes were spraying neat fuel down the fuel injection intake pipes, richening the mixture and causing the engine to be lumpy. Only when the fuel load dropped did it begin to produce its full, even power and Clark slipped into the lead only to have the race taken away from him when the gearbox jammed at the Tabac corner. In Belgium, despite a dodgy gearbox, he won for the second year. In Holland Clark had his celebrated battle with the police, but in the race he led from start to finish. Two wins in three races.

By now, too, Indianapolis was behind him. After qualifying Clark was back on the third row of the grid and at the start was ready to use his gearbox to shoot through the pack in front of him. However, this was not to be for Jim Hurtubise, the man directly ahead on the grid missed a gear and Clark almost rammed him. So at the end of lap one, instead of being third or fourth he was down in eleventh or twelfth place. But the Lotuses needed fewer pit stops than the traditional Indy cars and they took the lead. However, in a spate of accidents Clark was obedient to rules about passing when the yellow accident light was showing, as he read them, and by so doing he lost out to Parnelli Jones who used these periods for his pit stops. Jones ran out the winner, although his car leaked oil profusely – some agreed that he should have been black-flagged for this, as had another driver in the race for the same fault, but nobody acted, and the records show that Jones won and that Clark was second. Clark learned his lessons and, as after the South African Grand Prix the previous year, he determined to do something about it.

So, Indy impressed him in some ways, but he found the publicity difficult to stomach. He was not the easiest person in the world in his dealings with the Press – he was suspicious of their motives and didn't like inaccuracy in reporting. This led to odd skirmishes from time to time, and although he learned to live with this facet of the sport, he always found Indianapolis a bit of a chore for him in that respect. He once remarked that Indy would be ". . . fine without the Americans," but in time he made a number of friends over there.

If Indianapolis was a disappointment he managed to get his own back that season when he competed in the Milwaukee 200, a race for Indianapolis cars on a one-mile oval track. It counted in the U.S.A.C. Championship but was a race of no significance whatsoever in Britain. However, when Clark went out and won it, lapping all the conventional Indianapolis roadsters save A. J. Foyt's, the celebrated American chassis designer A. J. Watson predicted that the writing was on the wall for the front-engined Offenhausers.

Back in Europe the French Grand Prix was run down

the long straights of Rheims. Clark pulled out a lead of no less than three seconds on the first lap, but soon his Lotus appeared to be down on power. A combination of skilled driving and craft during a rain shower helped Clark hold the lead to the end – with two broken valve springs in his Climax engine he might have counted himself lucky to finish at all. Luck must always play a part in Grand Prix racing and luck was going Clark's way in 1963. At Silverstone the car wasn't handling right but he brought it home ahead of John Surtees to win his fourth Grand Prix in a row. Luck played a major part for Clark in the German Grand Prix, even though at the 'Ring Clark's winning run was broken by John Surtees. His Lotus was misfiring, yet Clark, using all his skill on a circuit which suited his style of driving, kept the car in second place behind John Surtees to maintain his generous points advantage in the Championship table. The decider, if all went according to plan, was to be at Monza in the Italian Grand Prix in September.

To a professional racing driver Monza is a relatively simple circuit, where power is all important. In recent years it has been a regular stamping ground for Ferrari, and the red cars of Italy have usually started as favourites. Such was the case in 1963 with John Surtees in pole position on the grid with his Ferrari. Clark made a good start and led to the first corner but in the back part of the circuit, through the tree-lined Lesmo curve and the flat and open Vialone, both Hill and Surtees got past with Dan Gurney on their tail. This quartet dominated the early part of the race, with Ginther's B.R.M. close behind. When Surtees took the lead Clark tucked in behind him to get every benefit from the tow down the fast sections, and there he stayed until Surtees retired on the eighteenth lap with a blown engine. This left Clark without a tow and Hill and Gurney began to catch him again and then they passed him. If Clark was to win the World Championship, it appeared as though it wouldn't come to pass in this race. But then Hill's car developed clutch trouble and he retired (which put him right out of the running for a second World Championship) and Gurney's fuel pump failed, leaving Clark in the lead once more, but yet again he dropped back, though this time he didn't fear another attack as Ginther was a lap behind him. It was just a matter of staying in front and hoping. Finally it was all over, the flag came down, the race and the Championship were his. An ambition was fulfilled, another mountain climbed. But already another one was in sight – Indianapolis.

The scenes at Monza were quite fantastic – an Italian might have clinched the title. In their enthusiasm the crowd jumped the barriers and crossed the circuit while other finishers were still running (in the mêlée the Reg Parnell mechanics tried to calm down some of the crowd with a bucket of water). For Clark, however, the victory had a bitter-sweet flavour, for on the following day, he was taken away to be questioned yet again about the Trips accident of two years before, an interrogation which was harrowing and took much of the lustre from his crowning moment.

There were three more races during the season – even with the Championship settled there was no let up. In the U.S. Grand Prix Clark was delayed a lap and a half with a dud battery, yet he finished third to Graham Hill and Richie Ginther. In the Mexican Grand Prix he further confirmed his 1963 superiority by leading Jack Brabham across the line. In the final event, the South Africa Grand Prix, he again walked away with the race and in so doing set a new record with an astonishing seven Grand Prix wins in one season.

By 1964, Jim Clark's racing seasons were following a strict pattern which included all the Formula I events and Indianapolis.

He also drove the Lotus 30 sports car in a number of races but neither this car, nor the Lotus 40 which followed it, were ever fully developed. Clark had little success with them, and was never quite happy with them.

The winter of 1963/64 was spent quietly on the farm sorting out the various problems of the day and getting down to planning for the following season. A new Formula 2 came into force in 1964 and, as usual, he went down to Pau to open the European season, and he opened it with a win. The early part of the season saw hectic preparations, however, for the Indianapolis 500 and the Monaco Grand Prix were run close together which gave rise to a number of problems, especially in trans-Atlantic commuting. Clark recorded pole position at Indianapolis but the race was an unhappy one. There was the terrible pile-up when Dave McDonald and Eddie Sachs lost their lives, and the race was stopped and restarted. Then Clark had trouble and retired when a tyre burst and the suspension collapsed, the car rolling to the infield where it came to rest. All the effort, the travelling and the mental strain had been for nothing . . .

Throughout, the 1964 season was one of those up and down years in racing when nothing seemed to go right all the time. At Monaco, Clark once again retired when his car lost all its oil, but he was again encouraged in the Dutch Grand Prix, when he won the race for the second successive year to "catch" Hill in the World Championship. Little did he know at the time, but the man who finished second in Holland, John Surtees (Ferrari), was to be his shadow during the season.

Things looked even brighter for Clark when he took the Belgian Grand Prix – his third successive Belgian victory – and established a clear lead in the points table. This win was really the biggest piece of luck Clark had in his entire career, as during the last two laps his main rivals dropped out of the race one by one leaving him an unknowing and astonished winner – particularly as he ran out of fuel on the slowing down lap and stopped beside Dan Gurney, who had also run out of fuel. They chatted about the race and when Clark heard the announcement that he had won, he just couldn't believe it. In the next race, however, the boot was on the other foot, when Gurney won the French Grand Prix at Rouen and Clark retired with a blown-up engine after he had built up a 15-second lead (this, incidentally, was the first win in a Grand Prix for a Brabham car built by Jack Brabham).

The British Grand Prix was another Clark race. After the last practice session at Brands Hatch, a little episode took place, partly through Clark's influence: Jackie Stewart, then an up-and-coming driver, was given a trial in a Formula I Lotus. He was quick but he tipped a valve when he missed a gear and that was that. Later on that season Stewart signed for B.R.M., though the indications had been that he would join Lotus and race with Clark.

At this stage the Championship seemed to be progressing quite normally and it looked as if Clark would pull off a second win. He had a healthy lead over Graham Hill and opponent Surtees wasn't even in the running – he was not among the first four. But the Nürburgring and the German Grand Prix changed all that, for Surtees won the race for Ferrari and Clark failed to add to his score. Graham Hill's second place for B.R.M. lifted him into the lead and Surtees quietly moved into third place. Unlike the previous year it was obvious that the 1964 World Championship was going to be battled out right to the very end of the season. The three leaders cooled their heels at the Austrian Grand Prix, because mechanical attrition on the rough Zeltweg circuit sidelined all of them, leaving the race to Ferrari's Lorenzo Bandini.

Now there were only three races to go, the first the Italian Grand Prix at Monza. Here Hill was out on the first lap and Clark pushed his car too hard and blew a piston. Suddenly the picture had changed for Surtees had come within two points of Clark and four of Hill. Graham won the American Grand Prix and Surtees took second place. Simple permutations of the possible scores the three drivers could count showed that the Mexican Grand Prix would be decisive. Hill had perhaps the easiest task as he only needed a third place to secure the title and Clark was suffering a run of bad luck. This, however, seemed to make little difference for he shot out in front in Mexico and led for most of the race. Hill had a collision with Bandini which sent the British driver red and furious into the pits to leave the race between Surtees and Clark. All the way Clark appeared to have it in the bag but Dame Fortune struck in the cruellest way as, on the last lap, when he was leading the race, his engine seized, letting Dan Gurney take the lead, followed by Bandini and Surtees. For Surtees to beat Graham Hill's total he had to finish second; the Ferrari pit responded to this dramatic last-minute change, Bandini moved aside to let his team mate through to gain not only the World Championship for himself but also for Ferrari the Manufacturers' Championship. This was a tremendous achievement as Surtees had worked long and hard to get the Ferraris 'right'. So Clark's World Championship lasted only one year; he was back in the pack, hungry for 1965.

Though 1964 had been an unhappy year in many ways there was an important consolation. In the Queen's Birthday Honours in June, Jimmy was awarded the O.B.E. for his services to sport. His was not the first O.B.E. in motor racing, but it was an honour which he respected and which was shared by his mother and father who went with him to the Palace for the investiture.

During the winter Clark went to New Zealand, returning early to Britain for some of the races which opened the European season, for the last season of the 1·5-litre Grand Prix Formula. In advance, this seemed as though it might be a season of anti-climax, but in fact was not, for

Grand Prix racing or for Jim Clark. He had the ideal season, winning six Grands Prix and retiring in four. He also took Indianapolis in his finest year in racing. Part of the reason for his success was the new four-valve cylinder head produced by Coventry Climax for Formula I. It was fitting, therefore, that Clark should dominate the racing scene because Coventry Climax thus had the satisfaction of underlining their supremacy in the 1·5-litre Formula and in their last year of racing. It was a tribute to their designers that they should gain so many successes.

The 1965 season opened with a bang, in the Race of Champions at Brands Hatch. Clark, scrabbling on to the grass in his hot pursuit of Dan Gurney, failed to regain the track and wrote off his Lotus against a grass mound. He stepped out shaken but unhurt. But more important races were on his mind. Above all, there was once again the clash of dates between Monaco and Indianapolis. Whereas in previous years there had been time to fit in both, this year a choice had to be made. Clark chose Indianapolis and when I talked to him about this he admitted that his reasons were not those generally bandied about. Most people said that he went there for the money and, if so, this was completely out of character, for money was never a serious motivation in Clark's racing career. Clark's own version was more calculated. Whether he went or not Lotus had to compete at Indianapolis due to their contract with Ford Motor Company. To Clark this meant that the Indy effort would be the most important and that, therefore, the Grand Prix cars might possibly get less attention. So he decided to go where the effort was going and do Indy.

Deep down there was this streak in Clark which dictated that he just had to beat the Americans in this race to show that he could do so.

After practice he found himself in the middle of the front row. At the start he confounded the pundits by taking the lead and the statisticians went to great lengths to emphasize that it was the first time anyone had led Indy from the middle of the front row. Be that as it may, his initial lead was short-lived as A. J. Foyt, the fastest qualifier, came past him on the second lap. Clark let him go and decided to use Foyt as a pacemaker. To Clark's disgust, Foyt began to slow a little so Clark repassed him to lead for most of the way to the finish. After the first pit stops he was pretty confident that he was going to win the race, for he found himself a lap ahead of the field. From then on it was a case of pressing on and hoping the machinery would stay together. This it did and Clark won the race, to be immediately engulfed in the publicity, the interviews and the fame which an Indianapolis win brings. With time to sit back and think about it, Clark credited his victory not only to the excellent pit crew he had from the stock car racing circuits, but to a simple petrol feed nozzle which Chapman designed on the spot, which allowed them to fill their fuel tanks quicker through the gravity feed pipes. That his driving possibly had more to do with it didn't concern him.

The writing had been clear on the Brickyard wall, yet nevertheless a world which had been well-ordered for years had been turned upside down. The introduction to the *Road and Track* analysis of the race set out the bald facts:

"So there was little surprise at Jim Clark's victory in the Ford-powered Lotus. The only surprise came over the ease with which the victory was accomplished. Clark led 190 of the 200 laps of the race and after A. J. Foyt's Lotus-Ford broke its transmission in lap 114, no one even threatened the little Scot."

By this stage in his career Clark had long since overcome his inhibitions about being inferior and not up to his role. He had become more balanced in his outlook and he had come to grips with himself. True, he still showed a modest exterior to the world and he still had his manners and mannerisms but, inside, there was a new confident Clark who well knew that he was the best racing driver in the world. This emotion he controlled particularly well.

Meanwhile, back on the Grand Prix circuits, Clark had opened the season with a win in the South African Grand Prix with Graham Hill in third place. At Monaco, Hill drove a fantastic race to win for the third successive year; thus he took the lead in Championship with Surtees tieing in points with Clark. The same trio out again for bear . . .

Clark's first European Grand Prix was once again at Spa and here he had trouble in practice. He also had a new opponent, the extrovert Jackie Stewart, who was running number two in the B.R.M. team to Graham Hill. Stewart had not driven at Spa before and Clark went to great lengths to help his fellow Scot. In the race itself Clark took an early lead; Graham Hill dropped back with gearbox trouble on the opening lap and this time Clark's shadow was Stewart. In the pouring rain which marked the race Clark was taking things easily, very conscious of Spa's tricky reputation in the wet. He took care when passing back markers, and at one stage this allowed Stewart to pull back some time. It was typical of Clark that he should notice this and put in a couple of fast laps to get out of Jackie's sight again just in case Stewart might have designs on the lead. Towards the end, however, Clark found some pleasure in seeing Stewart holding second place and so the terrible twins began their association in the minds of Press and public with first and second places. His win also put Clark back in the Championship and, as if to rub this in, he led the French Grand Prix, run on the Clermont-Ferrand circuit for the first time, with almost contemptuous ease. Stewart again took second place and now he appeared to be one of the biggest threats to Clark's second Championship. As far as success was concerned, Stewart was in fact having a better first season in Formula I than had Clark in 1960.

At Silverstone, Zandvoort and Nürburgring Clark dominated three Grands Prix, though his British Grand Prix win owed something to luck and a great deal to his skill. His oil pressure dropped dangerously low; assessing the state of his engine and the overall race picture perfectly, Clark drove on the ignition switch, coasting through some corners in order to prevent oil surge running the bearings, while at the same time holding Hill at arms length. After the German race – victory at the 'Ring gave him a great deal of satisfaction—Clark's luck ran out and he failed to score another point in the three final races. But his total of 54 points was sufficient to make him World Champion for the second time, with Graham Hill in second place and Jackie Stewart third.

Flushed with success, an Indianapolis win and the World Championship by a convincing margin, Jimmy received an honour which was very touching and important to him. In September he was made a Freeman of the village of Duns. Though he was not a native of the Borders, having been born in Fife, the bulk of his life had been spent in the south of Scotland and all his friends were there. He had certainly brought distinction to Duns as he always had himself billed in the U.S. programmes as 'Jim Clark, Duns, Scotland.' One reason for this was, as he put it, ". . . they have a bad enough job spelling Duns properly far less Chirnside where I actually live." In a ceremony attended by many people from all walks of life in the Border community Jim was made a Freeman, an honour of which he was particularly proud.

With the 1965 season the era of the small engine formula ended and in contrast the 1966 Grand Prix formula was for cars with 3-litre engines (unsupercharged); as usual, no constructors appeared prepared and, as had happened in the last seasons of the 2·5-litre Formula, 1959 and 1960, Jack Brabham profited, this time with his own cars, too. For Lotus, the engine problems were aggravated by the withdrawal of Coventry Climax, although they did have a Tasman Climax engine which looked good enough to tide them over until B.R.M. could supply them with 3-litre power units. As it transpired, the link with B.R.M. brought little success. Only once, in the United States Grand Prix, did Clark win a Grand Prix with the complex, heavy and fussy B.R.M. H-16 engine – even so, this was more than

the B.R.M. team achieved! All in all, it was a dismal
season.

It was a season, too, of surprises. In the first event at
Monaco, Jackie Stewart confirmed the promise he had
shown in his first season by winning the Grand Prix with a
2-litre V-8 engined B.R.M. The cars and engines were a
motley bag. Surtees' Ferrari had a 3-litre V-12 based on
the former sports car engine, while his team mate Bandini
had a 2·4-litre V-6, Brabham had his new Buick-based
Repco V-8 three-litre whilst McLaren used a Ford V-8
and Clark made do with a 2-litre Tasman car. On this
circuit the smaller engines did not necessarily impose a
handicap and it was Clark who set the fastest time in
practice. But at the start of the race he jammed the car
in first gear and it didn't move. Once he freed the gearbox
he made up ground – no easy job at Monaco – but to no
avail as the suspension broke and he was out of the race.
At Spa rain swept the circuit as the race got under way
and there was a series of accidents on the opening lap.
Stewart and Hill both spun, Stewart landing in hospital
and out of the Championship race. Clark had one of these
infuriating confusions on the start line; he left the grid
at the back of the field and then over-revved in his
anxiety to catch up, so he too retired on the opening lap.
John Surtees was left to win for Ferrari, his last race for
the Italian team, for shortly afterwards he left them on
rather acrimonious terms.

The French Grand Prix gave Brabham his first win in
this Championship year, and was the first-ever Championship victory for a man driving a car bearing his own name.
Clark did not even start in the race, as in practice a bird flew

Clark's Le Mans-type starts were invariably brilliant. Here, at
Le Mans, he shows a clean pair of heels to the field in 1961

Familiar attitude. Leaning back in an FJ Lotus at Silverstone in 1960, and (*below*) laying back and leading Graham Hill in the 1965 Dutch Grand Prix

Clark's greatest drives, for
example in the 1967 Italian
Grand Prix (*above*), did not
always end in victory.
Whenever he did win,
however, he was exultantly
received by Colin Chapman
after his cooling-down lap
(*left*, at Indianapolis in 1965)

Disappointment is a part of every racing driver's life—Clark
being consoled by Peter Arundell as he walks back after his
first-lap retirement in the 1966 Belgian Grand Prix

Life was often fun, even on "flag-showing" trips. But this game, at a Ford Cortina launching at Cortina d'Ampezzo, ended with Clark slipping a disc

The two great Scottish drivers of the sixties, Jackie Stewart
and Jim Clark
Two of Clark's close friends-behind-the-scenes, Walter Hayes
(*left*) and Gérard Crombac (*right*)

Sponsorship tends to be very direct in France, and Clark was always amused to honour his agreement to accept a bottle of Perrier whenever he arrived back at the pits after a French race

into his face when he was flat out, giving him a monumental black eye–no more, as he held the car on its line even in his dazed state. I spent some time with him at the farm following this incident when the enforced break gave him time to concentrate on other things. For a start, he had put his name to a range of driving shoes which was introduced at around this time. He was also planning to write a second instalment of his autobiography but this never came to pass as at the end of that year his decision to live abroad spoiled any book plans.

John Surtees had appeared at Rheims in a Cooper-Maserati but although he did a lot for the team, particularly in making the car a raceworthy proposition, this wedding was not really successful. Later his name was to become linked with Honda, and has been ever since.

The H-16 B.R.M. engine had still not been raced by mid-season and the British Grand Prix, so Clark stayed with the Climax engine whilst team mate Arundell had a V-8 B.R.M. engine in his car. Again, however, it was Brabham who won and the signs were that, of all the teams, it was Brabham and not Ferrari which was furthest ahead and most reliable. Clark really tigered in this race but had to stop for more brake fluid and dropped to fourth place, so gaining his first points in that year's Championship.

At Zandvoort he scored only a few more points despite one of his most brilliant drives, fighting with Brabham all the way and at times actually leading him. A crank shaft vibration damper broke and fouled a water line, forcing Clark to pit stop for more water. Still he finished third.

Driving the same car in the German Grand Prix, Clark just didn't have the steam to keep in contention. He slowly dropped further and further back and finally, in the wet, made a mistake at Aremberg and went off the road.

At last, at Monza, the H-16 B.R.M. engine arrived for Clark and he quickly set third fastest time for a position on the front row of the grid. His H-16 seemed quicker than the works B.R.M., but on the starting line he faltered before finally getting going. He had yet another battle in mid-field but late in the race the gearbox gave out and once again he scored no points. Clearly he was out of the running in the Championship in 1966 and nothing was going to change the picture, even though with the H-16 B.R.M.-engined Lotus 43 he did win the U.S. Grand Prix at Watkins Glen. This was the only bright spot, however, as in the final race of the series in Mexico Clark's transmission gave up on the ninth lap.

Even the Indianapolis 500 led to a disappointment in 1966. He took second place to Graham Hill after two lurid spins in mid-race (although lesser mortals at the Brickyard were astonished that he should even race on after these), and right at the end was misled by pit signals into thinking he had won. In this race Jackie Stewart had again displayed his talent, actually leading the race before he retired (he was credited with sixth place). No-one, however could gainsay Graham Hill his triumph, for he had driven with splendid consistency to win after a monumental shunt seconds after the start had disrupted the whole of the race. (It was restarted after the debris of 11 wrecked cars had been cleared from the track.)

By now Clark was beginning to earn the kind of money most people expected of leading racing drivers. His attitude towards business hardened and he was spending more and more time flying himself from place to place. His passion for flying had begun some years earlier, during the Tasman series, when he passed his initial flying tests. By late 1966 he was a competent pilot and had bought Colin Chapman's Twin Comanche G-ASUT. (He had originally ordered a new Piper but this disappeared in mysterious circumstances. It had been equipped with long range fuel tanks for Clark's many trips but went missing when being ferried across the Atlantic for delivery. As a result, Clark took over Chapman's plane.)

During the winter of 1966/67, Clark had many things on his mind. For obvious business reasons he had chosen to live abroad for a year, settling on Paris where he had many friends. His first race in 1967 was the South African Grand Prix and this took place against a substantial change in the background to the Grand Prix scene. For the Ford Motor Company announced a project for a new V-8 engine to be used during the season exclusively by Team Lotus. This was to be built by Cosworth, and it was, in a race against time. This announcement by Ford was most timely from the point of view that B.R.M. were beginning to feel the strain of being the main spear carriers for the British Grand Prix teams. These Ford engines were not, however, to be ready for the first two events.

In South Africa, Clark and his new team mate Graham Hill had Lotus 43s with B.R.M. H-16 engines, virtually the same as those used at the end of the 1966 season.

Clark's car began to overheat and finally the fuel pump broke and Graham also retired early in the race. Others had their problems, too – and when Denny Hulme had to dive into the pits with brake trouble, local driver John Love took over the lead. Then he had to make a fuel stop and so a surprised Pedro Rodriguez won the first Championship round in a Cooper-Maserati.

By the time Monaco came round Chapman had decided to give up the H-16, as it was expensive to prepare and was still unreliable. He played a gambler's hand by giving Clark a 2-litre Climax-powered Lotus and Graham Hill a 2-litre B.R.M.-engined Lotus. This didn't quite work, however, and, when pushing hard, Clark spun at the chicane and dropped to last place. But he wasn't finished yet and began to pull through the field, giving one of those displays of tiger which one could count on from Clark when the occasion and the circumstances arose. He climbed right up to fourth place to join battle with McLaren, only to spin again and retire –once again Monaco was his nemesis. Out of seven starts in the Principality he didn't win once. This race was overshadowed by the fatal accident to Lorenzo Bandini who crashed at the chicane and was trapped in his blazing Ferrari. Denny Hulme won his first Grand Prix victory, while dogged perseverance with a far-from-healthy car saw Graham Hill through to second place.

In the Dutch Grand Prix the tables were turned. Clark flew in to see the new Lotus-Ford for the first time – because he was living out of the country Graham Hill had done all the testing. Practice was not without its troubles, but right at the end of the last period Hill put in some electrifying laps in the development car to take pole position. In the race he sprinted into the lead while Clark settled down just behind the leading group. Then Hill fell out with a broken camshaft and Clark leap-frogged the cars in front to take the lead, and held it right to the end. This was a tremendous start to the life of a new combination of car and engine; this victory probably marked another turning point in the history of Grand Prix racing.

At Spa Clark was magnificent, lapping at over 151 m.p.h. in practice. In the race he got off in front, while Hill was left behind with a dead engine, soon to retire. Just as things were getting interesting, with Clark leading and Gurney challenging Stewart for second place, Clark pulled in to the pits with a blown spark plug. He set out again in eighth place, but had hardly got going before having to stop to repeat the operation. The leaders were then well out of range, and Clark could fight back only to sixth place, while Dan Gurney won for his own Eagle team.

The French Grand Prix on the "Mickey Mouse" Bugatti circuit at Le Mans was hardly successful as a race; for Lotus it was disastrous. After leading the race both Hill and Clark retired leaving Brabham and Hulme to take first and second places for Brabham. By now it was clear that the Lotus Fords had the edge on speed and that the Brabhams were their most dangerous rivals, primarily by virtue of their reliability.

One of the Lotus problems was flexing in the gearbox casing and for the British Grand Prix this was strengthened. Hill's suspension collapsed in practice – overnight work got his 49 on to the grid – but Clark did his fastest lap at an astonishing 123 m.p.h. In the race he led most of the way – only Hill got ahead of him – to take the flag first. But Hulme was second and was leading the World Championship.

The Nürburgring's twists and curves have always been a challenge to drivers and, in 1967, Clark turned in a practice lap of 8 minutes 04·1 seconds – no less than a minute and a quarter quicker than Fangio's equally astounding record of ten years before. The Lotus-Fords certainly had the speed but did they have the stamina? Graham Hill's car had brake trouble and crashed at Adenau Bridge and as the race started he was involved in an incident which dropped him down the field. Clark took the lead from Hulme, but shortly after this Gurney passed him. The Lotus 49 had a flat rear tyre, also the front suspension failed, so Clark had to sit back and watch Hulme consolidate his Championship lead.

The Canadian Grand Prix at Mosport was a new event and although Clark badly bent the spare Lotus 49 (entered for a local driver) in practice, he still set the fastest time. In the race Clark got away first, Hulme caught him and pulled away, Clark fought back until a second downpour swept over the circuit. Clark got past the New Zealander only to splutter to a stop when the ignition of the Ford V-8 was drowned. This left Brabham, who passed Hulme, when Denny stopped for a visor, in the lead with Hulme as runner-up. The World Championship was now between the two Brabham drivers.

In the Italian Grand Prix we saw Clark tigering once again and he was again quickest in practice. In the race

Clark was one of several drivers caught out by the starter, whose role was in part usurped by Brabham. He led the race which soon settled down into one of those battles so often seen at Monza when cars are fairly evenly matched. Clark fought back to lead the race and he was joined by Graham Hill after Gurney broke a con rod. Hulme challenged and briefly took the lead, Clark regained it only to have a puncture and a pit stop to change the wheel. Normally this would have finished any driver's prospects of finishing among the leaders in a modern Grand Prix but Clark shot out of the pits and started to carve his way through the field from sixteenth, last, place. Team mate Graham Hill led for a long time, to retire yet again, this time with engine failure but Clark was now in the swing of a tremendous virtuoso drive. When Hill had retired Brabham had taken over – and his lead was threatened by Clark! Surtees, too, was in the front and, when Clark had to make another pit stop, this time for fuel, he closed on Brabham. Surtees got the Honda ahead and fought off a last corner challenge from Brabham to win the closest Italian Grand Prix in years. Clark finished a brilliant third despite two pit stops.

By the time the U.S. Grand Prix came around the Lotus Fords were just about right and dominated the race, Hill leading until his gearbox started acting up. Clark was waved into the lead, and crossed the line first with his suspension broken. But time had run out and although Clark won the last race, the Mexican Grand Prix, the Championship could not be pulled out of the bag.

Indianapolis in 1967 saw a sensational run by the STP turbine car of Parnelli Jones and only abominable luck deprived him of the victory he deserved. This device had drifted away from the rest of the field, apparently with such ease that new rules were framed to limit its performance in 1968! For Clark the '500' was not a success. He finished in thirty-first place just a few laps ahead of Graham Hill, the 1966 winner, so neither Team Lotus driver fared well . . .

So the 1967 season ended with a note of hope for 1968. For Clark his year in exile was due to end on April 5, 1968 and he was looking forward to seeing his old friends and his parents (during the winter they had visited him in Bermuda). Clark had also made an abortive essay into Stock Car racing at Rockingham (he crashed the car in practice and never completed the race). He then went to New Zealand and Australia to win the Tasman Series. On January 1st he had opened the 1968 Grand Prix season by winning the South African Grand Prix in a Lotus Ford. The portents were there, the car had the mark of success, but for Clark it was to be his last Grand Prix. It was fitting that in winning it he set a new record of 25 Grand Prix wins, beating Fangio's long-standing total.

From Australia he had gone to Indianapolis to try the new wedge-shaped Lotus-STP turbine car and he had been impressed. Then he came back for the Barcelona Formula 2 race, to be put out after an incident with Ickx. The following week came Hockenheim – "a stupid race on a stupid circuit" – and there the story ended.

Over the years I had many opportunities to watch Clark, listen to him and try to understand him. Though on the face of it he appeared a simple person he was in fact quite a complicated man. To my mind Clark had more of a superiority complex in the later years than the regular inferiority complex psychologists suggest is the motivation for most people who set out to prove themselves in motor racing.

In the following pages many of his friends and associates, all of whom were closer to Clark in the later years of his life than I was, describe their own feelings about him. Having known him for so long, I was able to see the changes which motor racing wrought in him – above all, he appeared to become more composed, more at ease than ever before. He carried the confidence of someone who had found his niche in the world. There was no doubt but that Clark would have continued racing until the moment came when he began to be beaten. The farm was no longer the focal point in his life, and I had the impression that he was caught on this Hindu wheel of life called motor racing and that he couldn't get off.

He liked the travelling and the glamour – he thrived on it. Where he finally would have settled down I don't know, but he had financial security and could have settled literally where he wished. Though to the end he was still a kindly person to those whom he allowed into his confidence, he occasionally displayed a petulance and spite which was generally uncharacteristic. To some people he was cruel, but amidst this cruelty one felt that Clark was trying to punish himself for being unable to explain himself. Indeed, if he had an unfulfilled wish, it was to be understood by everyone, but to ask that was to ask for the impossible.

Everyone forgives his flaws for they were not serious

and he will be remembered more for his attributes. His love of children and the secret joy he had when, on promotion campaigns for the Scalextric firm, he would be beaten by the local kids. At one time he had a drawer full of watches which had been presented to him and which he was keeping to give to his nephews and nieces. He had many girl friends, who came into and drifted out of his life; to one or two he became very attached and there were times when one felt that he might have been happy to settle down and have a stack of kids. To the end he maintained that he would not marry while he still raced.

In Jim Clark motor racing had a superb ambassador because he was a proud person and a polite one. He demanded little and rewarded those who believed in him and had faith in him with a friendship which survived the passage of time and will be remembered by all who had the pleasure of knowing him.

The Formative Years
– Ian Scott Watson

The road to the top in motor racing is never easy and many contenders never arrive there. Twenty years ago money was more important than ability but with the commercialisation of motor racing the reverse is possibly true. There is perhaps no better example of this than Graham Hill, who started from nothing at all to become not only World Champion in 1962 and Indianapolis winner in 1966, but also a man of considerable wealth. All this through motor racing and his tremendous ability. In the same way Jim Clark started from literally nothing – in the early days he had no support whatsoever from his parents in following his career and, indeed, it has been suggested that Jim's father wisely kept down his pocket money as a further deterrent. So it was left to others, and in particular to Ian Scott Watson, to give Clark his start in racing.

It would be wrong to see in Scott Watson the image of a wealthy farmer lashing out money in order that Clark should race, as in the beginning it was all very casual and money really didn't enter into it. Scott Watson himself raced and rallied and, like most people who do, he dreamed of the day when he would be successful. Unfortunately for him, he befriended Jim Clark and very quickly realised, perhaps a little sadly, that it was no use dreaming of a career in racing when someone so talented yet so inexperienced was able to beat him so easily.

The early years of his relationship with Clark were idyllic for Scott Watson. He was elated to be able to put all his will into getting this young driver's career off the ground. But there came a split around the end of 1960 which left Scott Watson sadly disillusioned with racing and the people in it . . .

In 1960 he was left on the shelf while Jimmy set off on the final leg to greatness, with others to help and guide him. For Scott Watson it was a period of bitterness, but this subsided over the years and he remained a staunch Clark supporter. In leaving Scott Watson out in the cold when, in fact, Scott Watson had pushed Clark on when Clark himself wanted to get off the roundabout, we can possibly feel that Clark committed his unkindest act. Indeed, one wonders if this was one of the few flaws in Clark's character, for the indications are that Scott Watson committed the one major sin in Clark's book – he pushed him too hard. Whether it was in business or even in casual acquaintance with a girl, Clark hated to be dictated to. Elsewhere Walter Hayes recalls that nobody told Clark anything; possibly, then, Clark felt that Scott Watson pushed him too much but, whatever the reason, there was a misunderstanding and they never became close again. This was a great pity, for possibly Clark never knew how hard he had hit Scott Watson.

Down in the Moorfoot Hills south of Edinburgh, on the road to the little village of Greenlaw, where the local garage owner used to park his bright yellow veteran

Renault on the forecourt whenever there was a Charter-hall race meeting in the old days, there lies the land surrounding Harelaw farm, one of the two owned by the Scott Watson family. In the days when Scott Watson first met Clark his widower father stayed with his two sons Ian and George at Easter Softlaw farm. In 1958 he died and Scott Watson missed seeing Clark race abroad for the first time as he had to fly home on hearing the news. Later, when the estate was settled, crippling death duties forced Scott Watson to sell off part of his farm and in what remains of it he now lives in a modern house he designed himself. He has a natural flair for architecture and has developed with a friend in Kelso the Border Design Centre; he was also instrumental in designing the Ingliston racing circuit and is a member of the board of Scotcircuits Ltd., who hold the lease for the circuit and financed its construction. As he did with Clark in the early days, Scott Watson has now ploughed his enthusiasm into this circuit. Though he still farms to a smaller degree, his Border Design Centre business has kept him busy and one imagines that this, really, is what he always wanted to do.

Back in the beginning, he was younger, more enthusiastic and rather noted for the speed at which he travelled the Border lanes in a variety of cars. Indeed, in the mid-fifties he owned a number of DKW Sonderklasse models in a row and usually had at least one lurid incident in each until he was finally hospitalised. He recalls now that on this occasion he was in the next bed to a typical accident-prone local farmer. Everything happened to this man. Nearly everything he did resulted in an accident and a few months after leaving hospital he was killed in a car crash. Possibly Scott Watson got the message and ever since has driven with more skill and much less drama. While still in the flush of youth, however, he first heard about a young local farmer who was tearing around the farm roads:

"I first heard about Jimmy at the Young Farmers Club shortly after he joined at 17. The stories used to go around about this nutcase called Clark who drove around the Borders like a maniac. I knew the family slightly as Jimmy's grandfather had farmed beside us at Softlaw. My own father was a dyed-in-the-wool Border farmer and I think he was suspicious of these fairly astute Fife farmers, the Clarks, so he didn't have much contact with them.

"I saw a bit of Jimmy at the Young Farmers Club affairs but the people who really influenced him then were, I think, his farmer friends Oswald Brewis and Billy Potts, two friends he kept close to him until the end of his life. (Incidentally, it was with Billy that he did the Scottish Rally a couple of times as a navigator.) When I bought the Bufota, a Ford-engined Buckler sports car, he did a bit of work with me on the car. In the winter of 1954 he started to navigate occasionally with me in a DKW. Once, I think when we did the Heather Rally in the North of Scotland, Jimmy invented a new way of navigating, by laying the maps out on the back seat and kneeling on the front seat. The trouble was he shouted the instructions out for the way he was pointing which was looking backwards and we got into a whale of a pickle and got lost. On another occasion, during a Berwick and District Rally, one of the tests was a downhill freewheel through a ford at the bottom of a hill. Once through the ford the navigator had to hand the driver the ignition key for the driver to start the car and reverse back through the ford and up the hill. A snag was that the DKW had a steering lock on it so that if you took the key out it wouldn't steer. This led to a meeting of officials and they ended up deciding that Jimmy could leave the key in the ignition and freewheel down through the ford. He then had to take the key out, get out the car and hand it to me. Then I handed it back to him and he dived back into the car, and started it. He still set up fastest time!

"In those days Jimmy did a little rallying in the Sunbeam and I remember him once pushing me off the road on a forest section, he was going so quickly. He won the big Border rally twice, once with the Sunbeam and once with the Triumph TR3 which he bought later.

"The background to his first race is interesting because, although he has admitted that he had been interested in racing cars and drivers, he had never said anything to me about wanting to race. So when he came with me to that Crimond meeting in 1956 there was no thought in my mind or his about racing. I had entered the DKW for the handicap saloon car race and the sports car race, and I just took pity on him during practice and asked him if he would like to have a go. I already knew he was a fast driver from the events we had done together. I remember his face lit up and then we went into one of these sessions where he said no, he couldn't and I said he should and he said again no, he couldn't go out on the circuit. But finally he took my crash helmet and gloves and went out for the practice session. Well, he was three seconds quicker than me on his first flying lap and honestly, to this day I believe I was put off racing from that moment. It made me think then that I was a terrible racing driver and pathetically slow if someone could be that much quicker than I was. At this I said to him that he should race in one of the races and I insisted on him doing it. I entered him in the scratch sports car race and I drove the car in the handicap saloon car race. However, the officials came up to me and told me that I must have been running deliberately slowly in the saloon car practice for in practice for the sports cars I had been so much quicker. They there and then re-handicapped me out of the saloon car event and I realised Jimmy should have driven the car in the saloon car race and I should have driven in the sports car race.

"Around a year later we had formed the Border Motor Racing Club and Jimmy was assistant secretary. He played a big part in organising our first event which was a time trial at an old airfield near Beadnell on the north east coast of England. He ran my DKW and his own Sunbeam in this event and did particularly well. A few weeks after that we formed Ecurie Agricole and one of the papers came out with the headline 'New Team Challenges Ecurie Ecosse'. Our stock at that time was three Triumph TR2s, a DKW and a Sunbeam Talbot 90!

"In the beginning of 1957 Jimmy drove the odd event with my newest DKW, but it wasn't a successful car.

He came with me for the six hour relay race at Silverstone but wouldn't drive, for he felt he wasn't up to competing at Silverstone and by this time his parents knew he was racing my car. They didn't seem to take it very seriously, because I used to roll up at the front door with this very ordinary saloon and I'm sure they felt he wouldn't get far driving this car. By September I had thought about setting up something better for Jimmy to drive; a friend we had met at Silverstone was Michael Burn, who was then with Porsche, and he came up to the farm and with Jimmy and some of his pals we had a whale of a party. This ended up with me getting slightly drunk and agreeing to buy a second-hand Porsche from him. It was way beyond my means, really, and when Jimmy heard what I had done he thought I was mad. He kept saying we couldn't race *that* car but the following week I entered him for the B.M.R.C. Trophy Race meeting at Charterhall, the last meeting of the 1957 motor racing season. In three races, he was third in one, second in the next and then he won the B.M.R.C. Trophy handicap final.

"To my mind this was the turning point. Jock McBain, who ran Border Reivers, had not up to that time taken much heed of what I had said about Jimmy but after that race he decided we should get a car for him to drive in 1958. A few weeks later Jock telephoned and asked if I would run the team if he bought a car for Jimmy to drive under the Border Reivers banner. This was the white D-type Jaguar which had been owned by the Murkett Brothers.

"That season we didn't know exactly what events we would do but after Jimmy's success at Full Sutton in

his first race in the D-type, we decided to go to Spa for a
big sports car race over there. Part of the attraction
was that we could enter the Porsche in the GT race as
well. It was my idea and Jimmy was petrified at the
thought of it. Looking back, had I known what I know
now about Spa, I would never have suggested it. We
knew Ecurie Ecosse were going and Jock McBain telephoned David Murray and told him we were going with
the D-type – would David keep an eye on Jimmy and
not let him go and do anything silly? In the GT race
he finished fourth or fifth after a battle with one of the
quickest Ace-Bristols – and Jimmy was in the up-to-1600
class. I remember he was bucked to have been leading
Kurt Ahrens at one time, Ahrens then being well known,
particularly as our car was a standard road Porsche.
I, in fact, did not see the races as my father died that weekend, but in the big race Jimmy finished eighth.

"Jimmy's attitude to racing and everything never
changed in this period and there was no doubt he was
just a farmer who went motor racing; nothing else.
During those times it was a very hard job trying to get
him to believe in himself. About every second week he
would announce that he was going to pack it all up and
you would have to talk him into one more race. By good
luck in most instances he would win and everything
would go right. I remember once he went to Full Sutton
in the wet and drove a wonderful race which Francis
Penn reported in *Autosport*, likening Jimmy to the former
great Scottish driver Ian Stewart. That bucked Jimmy
up no end and made him carry on a little bit longer.
It was a question of running from event to event . . .

"Towards the end of 1958 we had thought of getting rid of the D-type and buying a Formula 2 Lotus, but after a trial at Brands Hatch, when Jimmy went extremely quickly, Graham Hill took over the car and a wheel came off. This deterred Jimmy and as at that time he remarked that he liked big bangers, we set our sights on something else for 1959. How we came to choose the Lister we bought I don't remember, but Jimmy had seen it when Bruce Halford drove it and he felt that it handled better than the big fat Lister-Jaguars of that period. Brian Lister had been impressed by his driving and I think he suggested we try to get the Halford car. Afterwards, Jimmy reckoned that if it had brakes it would have been a truly fabulous car (it didn't have any brakes because everything got so hot the oil seals melted, letting oil on to the discs).

"Even that year he got into the doldrums and was only bucked up when at Aintree in the sports car race before the Grand Prix he did so well in the wet against Stirling Moss and Graham Hill. His first Le Mans that year was also a highlight, for he was really in amongst the big timers. It was also his first meeting with John Whitmore, with whom he became very friendly, later on using his London flat.

"By now Jock McBain, who ran Border Reivers, was thinking in terms of a Formula I drive for Jimmy and, as he was very friendly with Reg Parnell, had raised the subject of an Aston Martin drive (Aston Martin were in Formula I at that time). Meanwhile, I had spoken to Colin Chapman on the same lines and it ended up with Jock trying to persuade Jimmy to go to Astons and me trying to persuade him to go to Lotus. In the end he signed for Reg Parnell because at that time nothing further had happened at Lotus. Later on Colin came to an arrangement with Reg Parnell which was to allow Jimmy to drive Formula Junior Lotuses when he was free and even a Formula I car in events not on the Aston Martin programme. What happened is of course now history – Aston Martin withdrew from Formula I racing, while Jimmy joined Lotus and drove for them for the rest of the season.

"At the end of that season Jimmy was in something of a quandary. Much has been said of his loyalty to Lotus, but at the Snetterton Three Hours race at the end of that season Reg Parnell had interested Jimmy in the idea of joining Yeoman Credit for 1961. At the same time Ken Gregory was trying to get him to join B.R.P. and both had offered the same money, more than he had been paid by Lotus. It was obviously a terrific temptation to him to move and I think he had almost made his mind up to do so. I got hold of Reg Tanner of Esso, who were sponsoring Lotus, and Colin and asked them to try and hold on to Jimmy as I didn't want him to leave the Lotus team. I felt he should stay loyal to Lotus even though by this time Jimmy and I had had our split and I was no longer concerned with any of his affairs.

"I spent the whole meeting badgering them over this, and meanwhile Jimmy was speaking to Reg Parnell and Ken Gregory. He had almost reached the stage of signing with Reg when I asked him if he would just hold on. As it happened Reg Tanner made Jimmy a new offer to stay at Lotus and he said he would think about it. Subsequently he agreed to stay. I was glad this happened for I honestly feel if he had signed for either Yeoman Credit or B.R.P. he would never have been heard of again. In those days the petrol companies had tremendous strength and once he left the Esso fold I don't think Reg Tanner would have let him in again.

"My connections with Jimmy didn't totally end in 1960 for when Scotcircuits was formed to build and promote the Ingliston circuit up in Scotland Jimmy played a very active part, indeed his Trust was the major shareholder in the company. Jimmy was particularly interested in Ingliston and played an important part in its development.

"For me it was a terribly difficult time and obviously I was very upset that this split had come with Jimmy. It never affected my faith that he would become World Champion one day, but in general terms I became very disenchanted with racing and I only went to about three meetings in the following season.

"I don't think I ever dictated, for instance, race tactics to Jimmy and I always left him to make up his own mind. You could never tell Jimmy to do anything and I think I probably made the odd mistake now and again by forgetting this and trying to force a decision on him. Indeed I think this may have been the cause of the split because I had tried to over-ride his occasional reluctance to come to a positive and expedient decision."

Team Mate
– Graham Hill

On the first day Jim Clark tried out a single-seater racing car he shared the track with Graham Hill. This was at a practice session run by Lotus at Brands Hatch in 1958 and on hand were the regular Lotus drivers, including Hill who was testing the then-new front-engined Lotus Formula 1 car. Clark had been introduced to Chapman as the possible driver of a Lotus Formula 2 which was to be bought by Border Reivers. Chapman had never seen Clark before but he was impressed by the young man's performance. His pleasure turned .to horror, however, when he found out that not only had Clark never been in a single-seater before, but that he had never even driven round Brands Hatch before. He was hurriedly flagged in and left to drive a Lotus Elite. Meanwhile, a few minutes after Jimmy stepped out of the car, Graham Hill took over and started to lap very quickly. Then the car lost a wheel and Clark took a sudden dislike to the idea of driving a single-seater and returned home to Scotland to make plans with Border Reivers for the purchase of a Lister-Jaguar sports car. This was his first meeting with Hill.

Graham Hill epitomises motor racing in Britain. He has the build, the bearing and the wit expected of a British racing driver and if someone were given only a description of what a racing driver is supposed to do and how he motivates people then that person could invent a Graham Hill. He is instant good humour one moment, and deep concentration the next as he prepares for a race. His humour is broad, it is puckish and it is sometimes deep, when only his eyes give away his intentions. He started from absolutely nothing but determination, and on that score alone has been outstandingly successful. Because B.R.M. had little interest in classes other than Formula 1, he has raced a wide variety of cars, too. Secure and in demand, he rejoined the Lotus team in 1967, just eight years after leaving it to go to B.R.M. He thus first met Clark the raw novice, he now came into partnership with Clark as a team mate, a fellow World Champion.

"When I left Lotus in 1959 I had been through two very unsuccessful seasons in motor racing – I had managed to score only one World Championship point. So I decided to join B.R.M. I had no idea then that Jimmy would be joining Lotus for the next season, so I knew him as a rival until 1967 and as a team mate only for the last year.

"Irrespective of cars, he was always a very competitive driver and very determined. You could never underestimate him as a competitor, because he was never a driver you could forget about if you ever did get past him. He would always come back at you – some drivers you can pass and you know that they might hang on for a few laps, but there are other drivers whom you know bloody well that you are never going to shake off. He was one of those. Invariably he was in front anyway –

in this his attitude was that of a killer, he built up a lead that sapped others' will to win.

"You have got to be aggressive in motor racing if you want to get on, and Jimmy was particularly aggressive. But he combined this with an extremely good sense of what not to do. One can be over-thrusting, aggressive to the point of being dangerous. This Jimmy was not, for his driving was always tinged with sportsmanship and fair play.

"In the cockpit, the excitement of racing lies in controlling the car within very fine limits. Motor racing is really a great balancing act, having the car broken away and drifting, doing exactly as you want it to and getting round corners as quickly as possible, knowing that you've done this and hoping that you've done it better than any other driver. You aim at perfection, without ever actually achieving it. But every so often you can say, 'That's it. Now beat that, you bastards.' This is the essence of motor racing. In this Jimmy was unsurpassed in his era.

"Character shows on the track, and more or less, people drive according to their characters. He was a tiger and had terrific spirit. That's how you had to race with him – you got as good as you gave. The time I pipped him on the line in the Trophy race at Silverstone I felt really sorry for him (although I was obviously pleased to have won). But it must have been terrible for him. He certainly saw me coming up fast on that last lap, because he shut the door on me. That's what he should have done, and he would have been silly not to have done it. But I went round the other side of him at

Woodcote – the chap who lies second on the last lap always has a great phsychological advantage, for he has nothing to lose and everything to gain, whereas the man in the lead has everything to lose. So being in the lead with someone right up your chuff on the last lap is particularly harrowing – I can imagine just how upset and disappointed he must have been to lose, it must have been dreadful.

"For he really had this great will to win, and I got the feeling that it hit him a bit hard if he didn't. It didn't last, was only a momentary thing. This happens, of course, to everybody, but with Jimmy it was easy to see – you could read his face and know what he was thinking.

"Comparing him with the great men of other periods is far from easy, but surely this is true: in their respective times, Fangio, Moss and Clark were the greatest drivers. Fangio was just that fraction quicker in a Grand Prix car than Moss. Moss was a better all-rounder. Then Jimmy. He won more Grand Prix races than any other driver, a fact which you just cannot refute. He won them all in Lotuses, and the combination of Colin Chapman the constructor and Jim Clark the driver was very strong. You just cannot divorce the two, it was a parallel success story. And Jimmy was happiest in Lotus single-seaters, which he drove in such a relaxed way.

"When people spend a long time working together in a game as involved as motor racing, then there is bound to be an affinity – I had a similar sort of thing going with Tony Rudd when I was with B.R.M. So when I joined Team Lotus in 1967 I recognised this situation, and I knew that I had gone into Jimmy's team; it was his team and I was the guest, as it were. But this worked out very well, we were both equal and I couldn't have had a nicer year with a team mate who was also such a close rival. In the team where the two drivers are roughly similar in ability one could have an uncomfortable year, and certainly not enjoy it. It is true that we were still rivals in the sense that we were both racing drivers and we each wanted to win. Not that I consciously went out to beat his practice times, for example – I just went out to try to get on the front row of the grid and if I did beat his time, that was it. You can't decide to come second when you are trying to get a lap time!

"Looking back, one of the nicest times I ever spent with Jimmy was in Acapulco, two or three years ago when we spent a few days there. We were away from all the fuss and noise and I got to know him much better. Two racing drivers are always on show and though you are friends there is still this little bit of rivalry. You always want to come out on top. After all if you are a competitive person it is going to show in more ways than one and this was so with Jimmy and myself. Yet there were times when we could get together and the rivalry would just drop aside and it was very pleasant to know him. He was a very modest chap and he enjoyed a good laugh. I will always remember his record and his ability, of course, but the little things you remember are his smile, the way his whole face lit up, and his springy walk and the way he bit his nails. He was an incessant nail biter, which completely baffled me; although he had a slightly nervous disposition this completely dropped when he stepped into a racing car – he was extremely confident in the car so therefore he wasn't nervous. Out of the car perhaps he wasn't quite so much at ease with people, or perhaps he wasn't at ease because he wasn't doing anything. We went on a trip from Frankfurt to Monte Carlo and back in a Ford Taunus shortly before he was killed, taking turns in driving. Whenever I was driving he was either biting his nails or fast asleep. When he was awake there was the occasional sharp intake of breath and the odd remark 'For God's sake, look out'. He was a very nervous passenger. It must have been particularly agonising for him to sit beside me doing 800 miles in thirteen hours or so. When he was driving and made the odd mistake he could never understand why I didn't say anything, and he used to say 'For God's sake say something'. We were just different that is all.

"His flying he thoroughly enjoyed and we both flew out to Frankfurt. He was so pleased to have got back into his aeroplane because he hadn't been in it for a while and flying does give you a great feeling of freedom. You feel very independent and there is a great sense of achievement. Again it is a matter of the control you need over yourself as well as the machine and this he had, which was why he enjoyed flying as much as his motor racing. So, we both flew in for the race at Hockenheim, Jimmy in a Piper Twin Comanche and I in a Piper Aztec.

"His Lotus for the race was very new – it had only been raced once before, at Barcelona the previous weekend, and in any case, its race there had been very brief, for Jimmy was put out in an incident soon after that start. I had driven it some 200 miles in tests at Silverstone, and there were no problems with it at all.

"I was a few seconds behind Jimmy in the first heat at Hockenheim when his car went off the road on the fifth lap. All I could see were some tyre marks going off into the trees at a point where we were doing about 150 m.p.h. Although the track was wet, this was in a very gentle curve to the right that didn't really call for any driving skill to negotiate at that speed (it was flat out in the Lotus 48). Naturally I did not think for a moment that it was Jimmy who had crashed and was told only after the end of that heat.

"My car was withdrawn from the second heat and we went out to inspect the remains of Jimmy's car. A marshal said that it had started to snake, and then went sideways across the track and into the trees. It was just inexplicable, like Stirling Moss's accident at Goodwood in 1962.

"Of one thing I am sure – it wasn't Jimmy's fault at Hockenheim. Everyone was taking that curve flat out, and Jimmy was the best man in the race – the best in the world. In this he met all the requirements; he was a natural athlete, he had outstanding muscular co-ordination, he had rhythm, his judgement was excellent, and his reactions were very fast.

"In personal matters, he was not a great one for revealing too much, and he was a bit clam-like, which I think may have been a Scottish trait in him? He was canny, and didn't go around saying too much to people. Very often you found out he had been somewhere or done something, which you would never have known about just talking to him.

"When he first came into Grand Prix racing he was very much a boy, although he obviously had talent. Since those days he had matured, and you saw this most in his public appearances, in things like speech-making. At this he gradually got better and better; this happens with everyone, but with him you could see it happening. He came from a country background, a very natural background and the pressure in the motor racing world is pretty hard – it comes as a shock and is pretty hard to assimilate. You could still see, however, how much he enjoyed going back to Scotland, throwing aside the acclaim, and being just Jim Clark.' One of the things which stuck in my mind up at the funeral was when the Moderator-Designate of the Church of Scotland talked about him being back amongst his own folk. When I thought about it I thought how nice that was—I can't say the same thing and so it stuck in my mind. It must have been very nice for him to have been able to return to Scotland to his farm, to his friends in the village and the towns and to have known he was amongst his own folk. When I go back to London I can't very well say the same thing – in fact I hardly know the people who live next door and I certainly don't know the people who live across the street. I haven't got what he had up there in Scotland but as I've never had it I don't miss it. I thought at the time how nice it must have been and the advantage of coming from that way of life.

"When he was in America he used to find some of the more pushing people got under his skin and it used to make him even more nervous and irritable. If you don't like it and start fighting it, it just makes matters a lot worse. It depended on what mood he was in because there is a lot of tension, particularly at Indianapolis. There it is terrific, right in the glare of publicity. This would upset him and it would show because he couldn't disguise his feelings terribly well (that isn't a bad thing in many ways).

"It was a combination of things which made him special – only he seemed to have more of the attributes than any other person. There was no single quality which made him what he was, except perhaps his competitive nature and his will to win. He wasn't going to take second best, but he wasn't reckless. He had superb control over his machine and a very intelligent approach to his racing. He applied this to the technicalities and got to know how to explain everything to Colin.

"I always felt very safe when racing against Jimmy because I knew he wasn't going to do anything stupid or anything unsafe. This made racing against him a lot more enjoyable. He achieved just the right tone, just the right level.

"With the passing of any great sportsman there is always a gap left. It may close down through time to a niche, but the niche is never filled. Time can heal the wound but the niche is always there, and his place can never be taken.

"When the crunch comes the little things vanish. Nobody is actually made for their part in life and Jimmy was taken from his nice easy going way of life and literally thrust into the jet set. If you are not basically that sort of person – and it is difficult to acclimatise – then you are bound to come out in spots occasionally. This is the cross you have to bear for being so well known and so good at your job.

"After the funeral service in the lovely little stone church at Chirnside we went back to Jimmy's home, where his family entertained his closest friends. This turned out to be a much happier affair than I could possibly have imagined, and one of which Jimmy, I am sure, would have thoroughly approved. It was a most sincere tribute to him."

The Other Scotsman
– Jackie Stewart

It was only natural that Jim Clark and Jackie Stewart should be closely linked by the Press and in the minds of enthusiasts, if for no other reason that than they raced together so often, as the greatest Scottish drivers ever to appear on the circuits of the world.

They were called the Terrible Twins, the Poison Dwarfs and many other names. But at the height of their friendship they *were* inseparable, for example in America, where people kept confusing them (not altogether unreasonably, for they were the same height, five foot eight, of roughly the same build, and each had broad shoulders and jaunty walk). For Jimmy, the relationship was that of an introvert Scotsman with another Scotsman to confide in and compete with; for Jackie, it was a rewarding relationship based on respect and the realisation that Clark's influence had greatly assisted Stewart's rise to the top in motor racing.

While Stewart had the feeling that Clark was guarded towards him in the early days, in fact Clark was probably among the first to recognise the potential in Stewart, back in the days when Jackie raced at Charterhall as A. N. Other for fear his mother would find out his racing intentions. For Jackie Stewart the chemistry was different. His brother Jimmy had raced successfully until a

In 1966 Clark gained only one championship victory, with the
Lotus 43 in the U.S. Grand Prix at Watkins Glen. In the
first two years of its existence, he was the only driver to
win a race in a car powered by the recalcitrant H-16 B.R.M.
engine (above, in practice for the Oulton Park Gold Cup).

Above. Lotus Chief Mechanic Jim Endruweit chatting to Clark before the start of the 1965 British Grand Prix. *Left.* Clark before his first-ever single seater race, in the FJ Gemini at Brands Hatch on Boxing Day, 1959.

MICHAEL TURNER '65

Last Grands Prix.   On his way to victory in the South African G. P., his last Championship race (*above*), and the Australian G. P., early in 1968.

Clark leading his team mate Graham Hill and
Chris Amon (Ferrari) in the 1967 American Grand Prix.

series of similar accidents left him with a weak arm. On the advice of his doctors, Jimmy Stewart retired from racing, but not before his young brother had caught the bug, for Jackie had been embroiled in the furore of the pits when in his early teens.

Jackie Stewart had a chequered career in clay pigeon shooting and had reached the very top in this highly specialised and skilful sport – he was in the final selection for the Olympic Games team, only to have what he reckoned was his worst day of shooting ever and lose the chance of a place. He might have shot at the Tokyo Olympics in 1964 but for the fact that motor racing had by then intervened and, from the moment he set his heart on racing, he had allowed nothing to get in his way. Today, of course, he is one of the world's leading racing drivers. The weekend he left Scotland to live in Geneva, Jim Clark was killed; this was undoubtedly the greatest personal tragedy Stewart has ever suffered.

"I met Jimmy for the first time either in 1961 or 1962 when I had my first races with Barry Filer's Marcos at Charterhall, our local Scottish circuit. He arrived at the circuit in his father's Rover, I remember, having raced at Oulton Park the day before. The first time I ever received any advice from him was towards the end of 1963, after my first season with Ecurie Ecosse, when I drove the Tojeiro-Buick and the Cooper Monaco".

This meeting, in fact, was arranged at the time preparations were being made for Jimmy's autobiography. He had just won the Mexican Grand Prix and the World

Championship and I had to spend some time on the farm with him recalling the events of his career. On this occasion, I remember, Jimmy had agreed that I should bring Jackie down with me and to our surprise we found Paddy Hopkirk already at Edington Mains. Paddy was staying with Clark for the night before a local motor club dinner where they were both to speak. That evening turned out to be most amusing, for Hopkirk knew nothing about Stewart and Clark was in the mood to stir things up, and part of it was spent with Hopkirk telling this young Scottish driver Jackie Stewart how he should drive round Silverstone. Two years later the same embarrassed Hopkirk was to concede that he had a cheek trying to give lessons to Stewart but how was he to know?

As the evening wore on an aspect of Clark's matter-of-fact approach to motor racing was to be revealed in rather an odd way. Stewart, effervescent as usual, started a lurid tale about how he had driven both Ecurie Ecosse cars at Snetterton, and changing from one to the other, had mistaken the accelerator for the brake in the esses. Clark sagely remarked that of course he had gone off the road? But no, Stewart went into an elaborate description, with arm movements, of how he had taken the car opposite lock one way then the other to come through unscathed. Clark clearly was unimpressed by all this and remarked that, if he could get off with such a stupid mistake as hitting the accelerator when he should have hit the brake and still stay on the road, he obviously wasn't going fast enough to need to brake in the first place. Exit Stewart, puzzled.

As Stewart was doing comparatively little racing at this time, Clark appeared to be in a different world to him, but a few weeks later Stewart's link with Clark became closer.

"At the end of 1964 Ken Tyrrell asked me if I would like to drive in the new Formula 3. I remember telephoning Jimmy to get his views, asking him whether I should do this. At that time I wasn't really interested in Formula 3, or in any single-seater class for that matter. This was something I had firmly in my mind, I didn't want to drive racing cars – single-seaters that is. My idea of motor racing was to drive for someone like John Coombs, and drive only saloon cars or GT cars. So when Ken asked me about the single-seaters I began to think who I could ask for advice and this led me to ring Jimmy. For a start I didn't know anything about Ken Tyrrell, but when I put the case Jimmy said that if I wanted to drive racing cars I had to drive single-seaters. He then went on to explain that once I realized that I really wanted to drive single-seaters there was no one better to drive for than Ken Tyrrell, the one man I could start with and get a load of experience.

"It was around the same time I had arranged to drive a Lotus Cortina for Red Rose Motors and I remember Jimmy giving me all sorts of digs about not driving too quickly – the usual capers. But at the same time I am sure he gave me moral support precisely when I needed it. After all, 1964 was my first year in International racing and I needed a friend in the camp! That year I drove fifty-three races in twenty-six different cars and

I was just driving everything with wheels on it. They were all good cars and, on reflection, I think that Jimmy had a lot to do with that. If someone was looking for a driver I have a feeling Jimmy put my name forward. This was most noticeable when I was given a drive in the Chequered Flag Lotus Elan – I don't think I would ever have got a drive with this team had either Colin Chapman or Jimmy not put a word in somewhere.

"There was another telling incident involving my drive in the Chequered Flag Elan, when I drove it for the first time at Silverstone. I remember distinctly in practice asking Jimmy what the braking distance was at some particular corner (he was driving a similar Elan for Ian Walker). I had never driven an Elan before and honestly it felt dreadful, so I went up to him and asked if this thing always felt like that, and we talked about it. I started asking his advice about braking distances into some of the corners, in particular Stowe corner, but he wouldn't tell me. This I could not work out, I couldn't understand that someone of Jimmy's ability and prominence didn't want to tell me, a completely inexperienced driver, apparently in case maybe I went quicker. I did not know if this was the reason or whether he was just in bad form. (In the race I had a good start from the third row in the grid and I caught Pete Arundell and then Jimmy in the rain, when I lost it at Becketts.)

"This was a thing about Jimmy, he was willing to help you so far but you had to do something on your own. I suppose I would do the same thing myself.

"It was also at this time that I started to live in John Whitmore's flat in London with Jimmy. From that day on we called it the Scottish Embassy. For me this was the period of trying to get to know Jimmy and this was a major task. I think I'm quite an outgoing person and I tried to get the confidence of Jimmy but it took ages and ages and ages. Even after that year I don't think we got close enough for me to consider that I was one of his real friends. There were periods, in fact, when I just didn't know him – days when he became so introvert and tied up in himself you felt you were infringing on his privacy. I remember worrying whether I had done something or said something to make him just clam up but, in fact, this happened with a lot of people who were among Jimmy's closest friends. Indeed, I feel that the real bond which sealed our friendship was when I had my first Grand Prix season in 1965 and finished second to him in a number of races.

"One of my proudest moments in that season came in the Belgian Grand Prix when I finished second to Jimmy in the wet. I had already won the *Daily Express* Trophy Meeting at Silverstone in the Formula 1 B.R.M., but Spa was something special. The Scottish newspapers at that time had started writing of the 'Scottish speed twins' and from that point on the bond between us was much closer. We came closest together either in Australia and New Zealand or in Canada. In New Zealand and Australia the racing circus was more of a community affair, with wonderful water ski-ing, flying, and surfing interrupted by occasional motor racing. It was a fun time apart from the racing and, though many people thought Jim led something of a monastic life, I must say that out there he was a real swinger, living a very busy life.

"I think Jimmy's loneliest period was when he went to Indianapolis for the first time, and this is something I can understand, because Indianapolis must have been hell for him as everyone and everything is so very different. He was getting the sort of attention that he didn't want. American crowds, for instance, are difficult to deal with and this didn't go with Jimmy at all. Obviously he got used to it after his initial visit in 1963 but when I first went there in 1966 I remember his delight that he had another Scot over there with him. I drove a Lola and, of course, he had a Lotus but we were doing all the practice sessions together. We ate everywhere together and stayed in the same hotels together. In fact we spent so much time with one another that we became known as Batman and Robin – and I kept calling him Robin. This perhaps was a big laugh but it just seemed that wherever Jimmy went I went and vice versa. This, in fact, made Indianapolis more bearable for him and made it possible for me because, without his prior experience, from which he passed on the facts of what it was all about, I would have been in his 1963 position. I just wasn't as experienced as he – remember I had my first Grand Prix season in 1965 and here I was at Indianapolis in 1966 – which was all a bit much!

"I was thinking of these times we had just after I heard about Jimmy's accident and how it would affect us all in the future. I must say that the days afterwards and around the time of the funeral were the saddest in my life. I was more upset by that than I have ever been over anything. You work out how it is going to affect you and where you are going to miss him, and, of all the race circuits, certainly Indianapolis was the first place which came into my mind.

"I get on terribly well with most of the drivers but somehow there was this different bond with Jimmy – it was deeper and more meaningful. Beyond our purely personal friendship, we were involved in many things together, even in our business arrangements, which were handled for both of us by Chris Weir and Jimmy Lyon.

"More than anything else I honestly feel that the fact we were both Scottish had a lot to do with our particular relationship. Even though Jimmy lost some of his Scottish accent when he was motor racing this was partly because, in some parts of the world, people just couldn't understand what he said, which is normal with everyone who goes abroad. In fact, in America someone listening to Jimmy and I talking between ourselves said he couldn't understand a word we were saying. It all became a garbled Scottish plot. We even had these problems in Australia and New Zealand, where our names would be mixed up, people would call me Jimmy Stewart and him Jackie Clark and so on.

"Jimmy Clark was also very nationalistic, indeed we both had this trait and we were quite sincere about it. It really had to be Scottish. If anything came up wherein he was called English he was at pain to correct it. What I think annoyed Jimmy was the insinuation back home that he was being unpatriotic when he decided to live abroad, something which I too faced when I decided to leave Scotland and live in Geneva.

"Jimmy just didn't want to talk about this as he felt it was nothing to do with anyone else. And he would not talk about it. Now he got off with this, and he got off with it by being pretty abrupt to the Press, and they didn't like this because they couldn't get a quote. I couldn't get off with it, for the second one never does. In motor racing there have been no people more nationalistic than Jimmy and myself, and if those people in Scotland who criticised Jimmy for what he did, or who criticise me now for what I am doing, were to watch Jimmy or myself on a parade lap before a Grand Prix where literally thousands of Scotsmen shout their heads off, they would get a different side of the picture. After you have won a race in Australia, New Zealand, South Africa or Canada the number of Scotsmen who come up to you is amazing. Scots people are more prone to be proud of their heritage than anyone else and this was epitomised in Jimmy, for to him it was very important that he was Scottish.

"When reflecting on the future that Jimmy had in store I feel that he was not going to go back to full-time farming in Berwickshire. He was living the life of an international figure and no matter what might have happened in later years, I don't think he would have returned to Duns permanently. He had become a very sophisticated person. He played pretty hard and his tastes were very high and these he wasn't going to satisfy in Duns. I am sure he would have kept the house and that from time to time he would have loved to go back up there, but I don't think he would ever have gone back and settled down in the way a lot of people would have liked to imagine that he would. This just wasn't on and this is why, when people told me that Jimmy was thinking of retiring, I know that this was not the case. We talked about this a lot but he really didn't know what he wanted to do in the future. He didn't let anyone know what he was doing.

"In other respects Jimmy and I didn't agree. Some of the things he did I would never do. For instance, when we were in Bermuda last Autumn, Bill France, who runs NASCAR, the ruling body of American stock car racing, telephoned Jimmy and asked if we would both compete in a stock car race at Rockingham. This was something very specialised, a 500-mile race around an oval track (Jimmy had in fact tried a U.S. stock car in practice for a meeting some years ago, but had never raced in one of these events).

"I wasn't keen on doing a stock car race, or any sort of race, at that time because I was on holiday with my wife Helen – we were in Bermuda for three weeks along with Jochen and Nina Rindt at Jimmy's flat. Helen and I certainly didn't want to break up our holiday, we wanted to enjoy it. After a day of decision-making, Jimmy finally asked Jochen if he would go with him and they both packed their bags and disappeared. As it happened, he had all sorts of drama, he lost it in practice, a wheel came off, his engine blew and he didn't finish the race (so Jochen, his co-driver, didn't even get a drive). This was an example of one of the things Jimmy was not terribly professional about – in my opinion he should have recognised the pitfalls. Other people had advised him on the same lines as I, but he simply wanted to have a drive in that sort of race so he went and had a drive. The same was true of the four-wheel drive Felday which he drove in a sports car race in the wet at Brands Hatch. He didn't need to drive that car in the Guards Trophy but he did so because obviously he wanted to drive something different. Then there was the time he drove Patrick Lindsay's pre-war E.R.A. at Rouen quicker than Lindsay, who was used to the car, could drive it. That was an example of his exuberance because he drove bloody quickly in a car he didn't know anything about on an awkward circuit.

"In New Zealand there was a really funny episode when he borrowed Jimmy Boyd's Lycoming aero-engined car. Honest to goodness, you wouldn't have driven it the length of your driveway, but there was Jimmy thrashing it round Invercargill – we were all saying 'well, that's the Tasman series sorted out'. This sort of thing is fun, something we all enjoy doing from time to time, but I like to drive different cars on private test and I'm very careful when I drive them. With Jimmy, curiosity had the upper hand.

"This sort of thing he enjoyed, and indeed he enjoyed his motor racing so much that here he tended to be extrovert, whereas we all knew that in many ways he was an introverted person. Someone who was an introvert would never have driven these more odd cars, for he would have thought that everyone would be looking at him, but Jimmy was not afraid to exhibit himself in these cars. I don't mean that cruelly but, if he had been wholly introverted, he couldn't have done it – really, Jim Clark was two people.

"He was much more conscious of his personality than most people realised. If you went into a restaurant with

Jimmy he *did* want to be recognised as Jim Clark. He didn't want it from the point of view of people asking for autographs but, like any human being, he did want the benefit of the best table. In fact he was much more human in this respect than most people give him credit for. Most say he was so shy and enclosed in himself that he didn't want anyone to recognise him or play on his importance. But while he never abused his position in all the years I knew him, he was very conscious of carrying the 'monarchy of motor racing'.

"His most difficult task in life, however, was making decisions. It was completely incomprehensible to find that someone who was so accurate and definite in his actions in a racing car was so completely inadequate when a decision had to be made outside a racing car. The number of times we have missed dinner because the restaurants have all been closed because Jimmy hadn't made up his mind which restaurant we should go to are legion, and the same is true of movies. One story is so typical of Jimmy. We were coming back from one of the American races and driving along a road where you cross a railway line with a ten mile straight one side and a ten mile straight on the other side. Jimmy is at the wheel of this Ford Galaxie and he gets to the crossing and stops. He looks one way then the other and there isn't a train in sight ten miles one way and ten miles the other then he turns to me and says 'well . . . what do you think?' He wouldn't dare make a decision without all sorts of drama.

"The record speaks for itself. But even without it, Jimmy was in my opinion without equal. With a tremendous natural ability he combined craftsmanship with a mastery of race strategy. He was a complete gentleman to race with, so that in close racing one could build up an understanding of intentions with him during the race, in such matters as over-taking or slip-streaming on a high-speed circuit. For me he was the driver's driver, for everybody he was the complete racing driver."

Views at Variance
– John Surtees

The arrival of John Surtees on the motor racing scene in 1960 caused a bit of a stir because, though motor-cycle World Champions had entered the sport before, few had the obvious determination and ability of Surtees. He was a dedicated man who had reached the top in an equally tough profession and he was wary. He was conscious of the various bricks thrown at him in motor-cycling days and the apparent stigma of being a motor-cycle racer. Even today he tends to be very wary.

He first met Jimmy in Formula Junior racing when Surtees drove a Cooper and Jimmy a Lotus. After a few spirited battles Surtees joined the Lotus team and whenever Surtees was free of his motorcycle commitments the two of them drove together during the 1960 season. At that time they were quite close friends, Jimmy being John Surtees's best man when John married Pat Burke. Jimmy had known the Burke family from the early days of his motor racing as he and Ian Scott Watson had raced in a team of Porsches at Silverstone with Pat Burke's father. When Surtees did not sign up with Lotus for the 1961 season their paths separated. One has the feeling that there was still a strong bond between them, the kind of bond one finds between two drivers who start out in big time motor racing together in the same team although Surtees agrees that in recent years they didn't see a great deal of each other socially.

Of all the present day Grand Prix drivers, Surtees is possibly the most independent and secure. He has the strength of character to rely on his own ability to achieve the goal he is striving to reach, and his link with the Honda Company will, in time, possibly become one of the most fruitful marriages in motor racing. He is respected as a superb development engineer and, if some of his motor racing decisions appeared to discount this – such as when he backed the ill-fated Aston Martin V-8 engine for his Lola at Le Mans – his design and engineering knowledge has generally borne fruit in the development of Ferrari, Cooper and Honda Grand Prix cars and the success of Lola-Chevrolets in the Can-Am series in 1966/67.

In contrast with Surtees, Clark was not technically minded and, though many people felt that through the years Clark developed a technical mind, Surtees tended to disagree:

"I don't think Clark ever did have any great technical knowledge, right to the end. The more I hear from a number of technical people who worked with him the more I am sure that there existed between Jimmy and Colin the ideal situation, in that Jimmy had started with Colin at such an early stage in his career and developed with him. Chapman, remember, had not only driven cars, and driven them extremely quickly, but he was also technically minded. With this background he understood Jimmy's reactions to the cars and could interpret almost anything Jimmy described even though Jimmy didn't know what it was about technically. This is what made them such a strong team. Indeed I don't think that that kind of strength exists in many teams, or even anywhere. Usually you find either that the driver has to do most of the work or the engineer has to do most of the work, simply because the driver doesn't know anything – and there are a lot of drivers who really don't know anything! In this Lotus team then you had Chapman the interpreter, who was also able to benefit from Clark's developing skill and talent, step by step. Jimmy also had an advantage in being non-technical because he often didn't know what was going on, and so didn't honestly know that something was maybe wrong.

"There is no disputing Jim Clark's natural driving ability and the amount by which he developed it and we must give him all the credit for it. But, at the same time, it was a group team. Though on occasions he had his problems, I do believe there was a lot of strength in the fact that Jimmy had this confidence in Chapman, while Chapman had the confidence in Jimmy and knew what he wanted. In general terms, I think it is imperative in most teams that, if you are driving a car, you should know something about the actual development side of it. But at the same time if you get too closely involved this can become detrimental to your driving career because it takes time and worry, things that can be inhibiting. You really have got to have a good relationship between designer, developer and driver without doubt.

"It is certainly rare to find such a link as existed between Jimmy and Colin. Nowadays, especially, with so many questions of finance and politics in teams, it is a great advantage to feel that the whole team is pulling in one direction. Most people will have noticed that many of the drivers have changed round considerably, staying with a team a couple of years before going somewhere else. They are not only searching for a good car but the workings of finance and internal politics also play a part. I think it would be better if we could all develop both ourselves and our cars together; this is the sensible approach. Remember too, that personalities play a big part in motor racing and to knit a team together is a most important factor. I think with the Honda set-up we have spent at least a year just trying to knit together the basis of a team to start a serious assault on Grand Prix racing. As when I was with Ferrari, I have been forced to take the initiative with Honda, basically because I have had more experience in the particular line on which we were working – the development of a Formula I car. This may sound a strange reference to Ferrari, but remember, when I went to drive there they had a new team of engineers, so we all started from scratch. I think that two heads are better than one and if you can get the right relationship going you can improve.

"On the pure driving side the combination of Jimmy Clark and a car he had faith in was a very formidable one, because when he had faith in the car and the confidence that he had the edge, then he drove his very best. Jimmy was not a mixer – he didn't like to mix it – and if he didn't feel he had a slight edge somewhere I feel he got very agitated. This is my own summing up of him. I don't agree with the general view that he was invariably a tiger. He was a tiger, yes, when he knew nobody had any sharper teeth. But if he thought someone might have an edge on him, then he wasn't a tiger. I believe that in an even match, or with a slight edge, Jimmy had every bit of confidence in the world, but in a case of adversity I wouldn't say he was a tiger. He would tiger, for instance, in a race where he had a pit stop, as in the 1967 Italian Grand Prix at Monza, and he would come out and have a right go. In that instance he *was* a tiger, but remember he knew that the combination of himself and the car on that occasion was the fastest combination in the race anyway. If he had been really scratching for the lead at that stage, say fourth or fifth in practice times, then I don't think the same Jimmy would have emerged. I do not in any way intend these remarks to be detrimental, I just think that is the way it worked out for Jimmy.

"On the GT and sports car side he didn't have a car which was terribly competitive and he had little success. Everybody forgets that a car needs a driver and a driver needs a car and in the Group 7 races, when he used the Lotus 30 and 40, he just didn't have a successful car. Mind you, I had a feeling that Jimmy was not particularly keen on sports cars. He certainly wasn't terribly keen on driving in America, which is something I can quite understand. I remember him passing remarks about some of the idiots who existed there and the fact that the less you drove amongst them the better. I understand this well for there *are* a lot of idiots. Unfortunately, there are a lot of idiots who are also quite quick so it's not so easy to get away from them. The other big thing is that in

Grand Prix racing we all understand one another and we are members of a relatively small bunch of people who are able to drive against one another. I basically knew how I should drive when I was battling against Jimmy and probably he knew how to drive when he was having a go at me. This happens between possibly six or seven people, so we each have our respective confidence – to a large extent this is a very important factor in Grand Prix racing. When you go to the States for a sports car event you are racing against a lot of people you don't really know, while there is very little likelihood that you will be in the fortunate position of establishing a combination of driver and car that will enable you to disappear into the distance, as Jimmy was able to do so many times in Formula I.

"When I go to a Grand Prix race I tend to set myself a level which I think I can attain. This has nothing to do with the opposition, whether it be Jimmy or Graham Hill or anyone else. You must have the maximum faith in yourself for, if you reached the stage where you involved yourself in watching what one man like Jimmy did, it would mean that you didn't have enough faith in your own ability. If you do reach that stage I think you ought to stop, pack up and earn your living some other way, enjoy yourself some other way.

"With Jimmy now gone, Lotus can't be the same. It is a big blow to them for, if you have a very close team effort as such, as distinct from a number of individuals where the loss of a member doesn't matter so much, the strength of the first set-up is also its weakness. This relationship between Colin Chapman and Jimmy was their strength, but Chapman has now reached such a stage in development that it won't mean they will stop winning races. They won't, they will carry on and be successful, but you will not get that relationship again, for any newcomer coming on the scene would arrive at a different stage of development from that which existed originally between Chapman and Clark. Perhaps Colin's patience will be a little more strained than in those early days when he too was developing in Formula I.

"I was a lot closer to Jimmy up until 1963 than I have been in recent years. When we started we had quite an understanding between us but we had different temperaments and just seemed to drift apart. Jimmy's loss is not only felt by the people close to him like his parents and motor sport in general. Though I have mentioned that I don't believe in setting sights on anything, Jimmy did have this tremendous reputation. One of the dangers of having a reputation, however, is that everybody wants to beat it and Jimmy is no longer here to defend his reputation in the only way which is satisfactory – on the circuit. This is a great loss not only to enthusiasts but also to his competitors. Even if drivers believe they were better, they cannot now prove it on a circuit. I think this hurts all sorts of people, because it must be that the aim of anybody who has faith in his own ability is to get into equal cars and have a sort-out with the person who is recognised as being the best."

The Cosmopolitan Clark
– Gérard Crombac

For the last sixteen months of his life Jim Clark lived
abroad, either in a flat in Paris or in the flat in Bermuda
which he bought in 1967. The reasons for this are as
unimportant as they are obvious. For a high earner the
British taxation system, as it stands at present, gives little
or no incentive to stay in this island and for a person like
Clark, who in any case spent much of his time travelling
around the world, it was to his advantage to stay abroad
at least for a year. Indeed, one of the great tragedies
surrounding his death was that the weekend after the
Hockenheim meeting he had intended to come back home
to Chirnside to see his family. His parents had visited
him in Bermuda but they had not seen him for five
months and he did want to get home again and have a
look round.

Whereas in a racing car Clark was secure and confident,
there were areas in which he was less secure and when
the decision came to live abroad he chose Paris, not
because of its reputation as the 'City of Lights', but
probably because he had in Paris one of his closest
friends and confidants, the French motoring journalist
Gérard 'Jabby' Crombac who is editor of the leading
motor sporting journal *Sport Auto*. Crombac had founded
Sport Auto at about the time that Clark became an

international driver and always followed him closely – they often shared hotel rooms. This gained Crombac the nickname "Cromclark" from some of his fellow journalists.

Crombac's link with Clark came through the Lotus organisation for, in the early days when Colin Chapman was building up his empire, Crombac became his first foreign customer. The car he bought in 1953 was Chapman's own Lotus Mark VI (1611 H) which *Motor* had called the "preposterously fast Lotus". Crombac became their right-hand man on the Continent for, as he explains, in those days everyone at Lotus had problems with foreign languages and foreign regulations. Since then Jabby's links with Lotus have been strong and it was only natural that as Clark became involved with Lotus so the two of them should come together.

In 1959 Jim Clark and John Whitmore shared a Lotus Elite at Le Mans, where Crombac had entered another car of the same type to be driven by the French driver Jean François Malle, the brother of film director Louis Malle.

It was at this race that Crombac first met Clark as they were staying in the same little country pub about thirty miles from the circuit. Crombac was in the smallest room up in the attic, and Jimmy was in the next smallest which he was sharing with Ian Scott Watson. From there the friendship flourished, a friendship which was to exist right up to the end.

"He was very shy, I remember, and I don't think he spoke French at all. My attention was not drawn to him because of his brilliant performance or anything, for at Le Mans it is very difficult to judge a driver, but I have had many Scottish friends starting with Ron Flockhart (who was to drive at Le Mans later with Jim); indeed it was probably Ron who got me interested in Jim's career.

"In those days, of course, Jimmy was just a Scottish farmer who went motor racing. There was absolutely no glamour about him. I didn't realise he was a good driver until he drove the Lotus 18 Formula I car the following year for, though the British enthusiasts were able to see him regularly in these formative years, I only saw him at Le Mans.

"The following season I bumped into Jimmy again at Monaco when he was entered for the Formula Junior race in a Lotus 18. At that time I was acting as a racing manager – a kind of French Ken Gregory, purely on an amateur basis – running a thing called the Inter Auto Course organisation. We handled a number of drivers and I had about six or seven entries in the race, one of them a Cooper for the man who is now Carroll Shelby's team manager, Carrol Smith. Carrol was racing the previous weekend at Aix-les-Bains and had bent his car and so he couldn't run at Monte Carlo. The organisers however had refused an entry for Ken Tyrrell's Cooper at Monaco for the plain and simple reason they didn't know anything about Formula Junior and the drivers. Ken's driver on that occasion was Henry Taylor (who is now Ford's competitions manager) but the Monaco people didn't know his potential. I thought this was ridiculous so I went with Ken Tyrrell to see the organisers, only to be told that it was too late to issue a new entry form because the entries were allotted. It was then agreed that if Carrol Smith didn't turn up we could nominate another driver, which put the ball back in our court, and I had to enter the car under our team on Ken Tyrrell's behalf, so I entered Henry. As it transpired, I spent the race in Jimmy's pit and Henry won the race. In fact Jimmy Clark was walking the race when his engine mounting came adrift and the engine started shaking in the frame and this, in turn, shook a wire off the coil. It was at this event that I realised how quick Jimmy was, and I wasn't alone in this. Even though he was a Formula Junior team driver, I remember that Colin Chapman wanted to put Jimmy in the Formula I car for a few laps, because Alan Stacey wasn't faring too well in practice. He was having trouble, I seem to remember, in finely controlling the power of the car because he had an artificial leg (this also meant that he was unable to 'heel and toe').

"I probably got to know him better at Pau, because I have always been involved with the organisers there in arranging entries for drivers and I always tried to get Jimmy for the race. It was a race he liked because Pau is a very pleasant little town – a spa set in pleasant surroundings. Above all, the circuit is a little Monte Carlo and is a real driver's course. Through the years Jimmy really became the 'King of Pau', winning the race four times, and usually holding the lap record.

"After that I saw more and more of Jimmy – I was going to more and more races and Jimmy was becoming a really professional driver, driving in most major events.

"When later he decided to live in Paris his reasons were varied, but mainly he felt he had a lot of friends there and someone to help him find a flat. He also knew about the Club Sport Auto, a kind of Steering Wheel Club where French racing drivers gather for lunch every day (it is actually a restaurant beside our offices), and he knew he could meet motor racing friends there. Paris was convenient for phoning London and Edinburgh, for it was important to keep in touch with things at home. He also had some business in France.

"So in January 1967 he decided to come to Paris, where he lived in my flat. Though he was based in Paris, however, he didn't spend a great deal of time there, using my flat mostly for keeping trophies and things. When he did stay his schedule was fairly set. If he was there for any length of time he would have his advisors come in and spend one or two days with them. Then he worked hard, and could not be seen or disturbed on the telephone. But normally he would arrive at the club for lunch and afterwards would come back to the office and read through the motoring magazines. He didn't subscribe to all of them, but he was very keen to read everything that was said about him, and to make sure that there were no mistakes (this was a characteristic of Jimmy – he was most insistent that even the smallest mistakes should not be made). He would spend half the afternoon reading sitting on a chair half in and half out of the little office – we call it a *cabinet*, which is more nearly accurate – where we kept the British and French journals. Sometimes if there were too many people talking in the office he would even shut himself in it.

"So visitors would come into the office and come face to face with Jim Clark, sitting reading what, say, Denis Jenkinson of *Motor Sport* had written about him. He enjoyed the writing of specialist motor racing journalists, but on the other hand was not at all keen on the kind of sensationalism so often found in daily newspapers. Here in France he discovered, too, that the French daily Press is not terribly interested in motor racing and is much less aggressive than the British daily Press. This was a boon to him because he was very rarely bothered by them. In fact they never got his address, and one of my duties was to filter all the messages and queries which he was getting from all these journalists.

"One thing which upset him was all the fuss, and the praise he got, after his fruitless 1967 Italian Grand Prix drive when he made up a whole lap on everybody, and was about to win, only to run out of fuel on the last lap. He was hailed as the world's greatest then, but in his mind he had done nothing exceptional in this race. He did not think that Monza is a driver's circuit. If his team mate Graham Hill hadn't blown up he could not have caught up with him, and in any case, he knew that he just had a better car than anybody else. In Jimmy's mind, the best race he ever did was the 1962 German Grand Prix when he forgot to switch on his fuel pumps at the start, and in the end finished "only" fourth. This was probaby the only race when he drove at ten-tenths throughout, and in his mind the fact that he hadn't been praised for it was a severe criticism of most journalists.

"His social life was restricted mainly to racing people. He was very friendly with Jochen and Nina Rindt, who also lived in Paris at this time; in the club he met most of the French drivers in motor racing and the parties he went to were motor racing parties. He seldom went out on his own.

"He reacted quite well to living in Paris because he became addicted to French food. In a restaurant he would go through the wine lists and he knew something about the subject (one of his favourites was a red Bordeaux). He was no gourmet but he was becoming one, and as he was very fond of French oysters we usually ended up in a sea food place.

"One of the great driving forces behind Jim Clark was his curiosity about motor cars and his fascination with them. When I told him last year of a friend of mine who owned a D-type Jaguar his eyes lit up and he asked if I would find out if he could drive the car. My friend is a very wealthy man who owns a number of racing cars, and he even has his own racing track on his estate where he spends the weekends with his cars. He does a little bit of hill climbing too. His son of fourteen has a little Formula 4 racing car in which he goes like a rocket, and Pierre has told me that while because of his business he himself could not become a full-time racing driver, he wants his son to become World Champion.

"We fixed up a date for the visit and we all drove down in Jim's big Ford Galaxie last September. In addition to owning the racing cars, Pierre is co-owner of one of the great Bordeaux vintage wines so we had a wonderful time. He would say to Jimmy 'try this '62, I think you will find it very good'. We mixed our pleasures that weekend . . .

"The cars included the D-type Jaguar, but unfortunately the back axle was making noises and Jimmy therefore treated this car fairly gently as he didn't want to break it. There was also an old Delahaye, a Type 51 Bugatti and three different Ferraris.

"One of them was a P4 sports-racing car which Pierre had bought from the Fillipinetti team and it was this car which Jimmy drove most of all. It was the newest of all the Ferraris and it was race-prepared; needless to say, it was expected of him to break the lap record for this private circuit. First of all he took his girl friend round in the Ferrari. Then he told me it was my turn.

"It is a funny thing, I have often been driven by Jimmy and have got no impression of speed. I thought while we were going round that it was good of him not to frighten me, and when we stopped I told him it was very nice of him to take me round so gently—I was so sure he had been about five seconds a lap slower than when he took his girl friend round. Jimmy just laughed and Pierre came up and told us we had broken the lap record.

"In Paris, Jimmy usually drove his yellow Lotus Elan coupé, and he admitted once that since he had lived on the Continent he had rediscovered the pleasures of motoring. So he used his Piper Comanche less often, sometimes preferring to drive the Elan to circuits such as Spa and the Nürburgring. He had really rediscovered motoring.

"Jimmy wanted to drive the Indianapolis car on a road course, and in time he was able to do this. To my mind he was always looking for something which would give him the biggest 'thrill'. He looked for new sensations in motor racing and he enjoyed them. He realised that the Indy car could be more satisfying than most in this respect, as it was much more powerful than the Formula I car. It was brought to Europe for him to drive in the Ollon-Villars hill climb in Switzerland, but this was an experience he wanted to forget as they had difficulties with the fuel system and it didn't handle very well on the twisty course. He then had a chance to drive one in a race on the Fuji circuit in Japan, but here he had trouble too. Eventually he ran an Indy-style car last September in the Rex Mays 300 at Riverside. (The generous side of Jimmy was shown here, and widely quoted in the American press. After he retired, having over-revved the engine, he intended to share his purse with the mechanics, because he thought his mistake had deprived them of some earnings.)

"He would go to great lengths to do things for his friends and he could be very generous. The highspot of my career was watching Jimmy win at Indianapolis in 1965, and that year the well-known motor racing artist Michael Turner prepared a painting which was used as a Christmas card. This showed Jimmy ahead of A. J. Foyt. Michael hadn't been at Indianapolis that year and he borrowed some of my colour transparencies to get the colours of the cars correct. I was fascinated by this painting which was then hung at the Steering Wheel Club in London. For years I had been engrossed in buying myself a house, and I jokingly said to Jimmy that when I had finished furnishing the house and paying for it, I wanted to buy this painting as it represented my finest moments in motor racing. Suddenly, a few months later, he turned up with the painting under his arm. He had bought it for me. I only found out later just how much trouble he had gone to, for at that time there were two paintings of Indianapolis in the Steering Wheel. Jimmy knew the one I wanted, but as he was living out of the country at the time, he got Graham Hill to negotiate with the Steering Wheel for the purchase of the painting. Unfortunately, Graham bought the wrong one, and brought it to the 1967 French Grand Prix at Le Mans. I didn't know about this but he apparently showed it to Jimmy who realised the mistake right away. At this moment I came on the scene and they hurriedly shut the boot of Graham's car, so I knew nothing about it until the British Grand Prix at Silverstone when he gave the Turner painting to me.

"The same year the French Bosch company ran a competition where each Monday morning a group of French journalists would gather and award a 'spark' to the person who, in their opinion, had done best in motor sport in the previous week. At the end of the season he had collected more sparks than anyone else and the prize was goods from Bosch. They asked him what he wanted as the prize, and he said he would like a colour television set for his father to be delivered in Britain.

"But although he was very generous, he remained the canny Scot of legend and he was not one to waste any money. I remember that he didn't want a house maid in the flat, so if one turned up in the middle of the morning, one might find James Clark Esq., O.B.E., pushing the vacuum cleaner through our living room.

"Though Jimmy, through his racing, became a man of

the world, he remained a true Scotsman – he had an enormous love for Scotland and Scots people. I thought his rather strong Scottish accent was fading with the time, until an incident when he was invited to patronise the opening of a French pub, which was to be done in style with the help of a pipe band. When Jimmy turned up and realised these people were fellow Scots he started chatting happily with them and I could hardly understand what he was saying as his accent had come back strongly and so suddenly.

"Jimmy's Scottish upbringing had instilled in him a rather restrained attitude towards girls, and I think he was very very shy with them in the early part of his career. But he was also tremendously attractive to them – they would come up to him for autographs, and would leave no doubt as to their true intentions. In part he enjoyed this, but I also think he was put off in a way by this ruthless approach, so that he had absolutely no respect for most of them. So as a result, there were times when he wasn't the perfect gentleman.

"Once he was photographed in a nightclub with a girl and the photographer asked if she was his fiancée. He replied that she was just a girl friend and that he had plenty of girl friends. But at that time this girl really was his number one and I didn't think this was a nice thing to do. However, sometimes Jimmy got attached to a girl for whom he felt differently. I think Sally Stokes was one of the two, and for a few years, she really was very close to Jimmy, following him to most races. Needless to say, this was not greatly appreciated by the bunch of 'scalp hunters' who were usually on the trail of Jim as well.

"He also had this thing about not wishing to exploit his success in dealings with other people. I remember once that he had a tight timetable for getting from testing at Indianapolis to the Pau Grand Prix. His own plane was flown over to France by a friend and left at Toussus le Noble, a private airport just outside Paris, and to make sure he wasn't going to miss the Pau practice session, we covered the route from Orly to Toussus le Noble a couple of times in advance and he took pace notes so that he knew exactly which way to turn at the road junctions and cross roads; the connections were tight as that. I suggested to him that we should go to the Air France V.I.P. lounge at Orly and arrange with them that he could get to his car very quickly. I more or less had to drag him into it. He wasn't at all keen. In the end he was pushing it so little he got no help at all and when he arrived at the small airfield time was very short. I didn't know much about the fuelling arrangements of the 'plane and he discovered that only one petrol tank had been filled so there was another delay whilst the second tank was filled up. Eventually he arrived at the circuit and stepped into the car as the others were moving off for practice. Three laps later he had bettered the lap record.

"I think Jimmy remained the Scottish farmer for the whole time he knew only Europe and even when he took the odd trip to the States. Possibly the thing which changed him most was Indianapolis. In fact, I think that race changed him completely. Indeed at about the time he first raced there, a rumour that he would retire from motor racing got about; although he squashed this I did wonder if he had maybe thought about retirement. I wasn't close enough to him at that time to tell. I know, however, that he came back after that with a vengeance.

"I think I was the only journalist from Europe who followed every one of Jimmy's Indianapolis attempts and this I consider the highlight of my journalistic career. I always stayed with him and the first year, 1963, the trip was very much more like a crusade than just a trip to another motor race. The spirit was that all Europe was behind this, not just Britain or Scotland. It was Europe versus America. Lotus went there to win and should have won. But there was the trouble about Parnelli Jones spilling oil, not being black flagged, and so on.

"That first year we all shared the same room; Jimmy, Colin, Cyril Audrey, the time keeper, and myself. Jimmy and Colin had beds, Cyril had a separate camp bed and I slept on the floor with a blanket because we were simply not organised. At Indianapolis you really have to be organised—we didn't even know how to book rooms.

"What first made Jimmy uncomfortable about Indianapolis was the generally hostile attitude of some people. This was not directed at him because he was Jim Clark but at a foreigner coming to take away their money. They saw he was going quickly and I am sure this was the main reason for their hostility. I feel, too, that there was a certain amount of jealousy in America that a foreigner should be the first to benefit from the money ploughed into Indianapolis by Ford of America. That first year was very tense, although I must

Clark thoroughly enjoyed sorting out the Lotus Cortina in its
early races (here at Silverstone in 1964)

An opportunity to drive a "different" car was always welcome, hence this outing in a Type 51 Bugatti on a private circuit in France

Lotus Cortinas.   Three-wheeling exhuberantly through Bottom
Bend at Brands Hatch (*above*) and helping to heave his car out of
a ditch in Loch Ard special stage of the 1966 R.A.C. Rally

One of Clark's few bright spots in a generally dismal 1966 season came at Watkins Glen, when he drove the BRM H-16-engined Lotus 43 to its only victory

Familiar situations.
Clark raising a thumb as
he takes the flag at the
end of the 1967 British
Grand Prix and holding
up the trophy a few
minutes later

In mechanical matters there was an extraordinary *rapport* between Jim Clark and Colin Chapman. *Above* Clark explaining a handling problem at Monaco in 1967 and (*right*) watching Chapman found out how a turbine pump works during a night session at Indianapolis in 1968 *Left* Triumph and failure in America—at the end of the 1965 Indianapolis 500, and grimacing at bent metal after his only stock car race

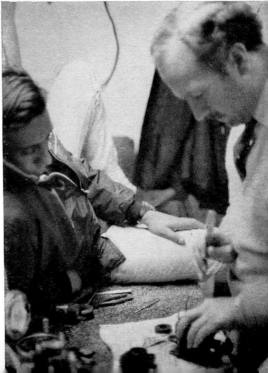

Another sort of driving—Jimmy at the controls of his Piper Twin Comanche, which he bought from Colin Chapman

say that it improved in later years as Jimmy was accepted and he became one of the group, friendly with everybody.

"In a World Championship Grand Prix there is a lot at stake, but it is only one of a series of races. Indianapolis was something different for Clark because financially he was earning most of his money in this race and the pressure was intense. As if this was not enough, the Indianapolis atmosphere was not compatible to Clark's temperament because some of the people used to bother him. I remember last year we were having breakfast before the race with Colin Chapman and Cyril Audrey – and it is easy to imagine how tense the atmosphere is at this time, so close to the race. Apart from the financial side, there is this oppressive thing about Indianapolis being something of a make or break race. If you lose you have to wait a whole year before having another crack at it. We were all tense, silent and staring into our corn flakes when a big woman barged in and said something like 'Hello Jimmy, my name is so and so, pleased to meet you'. She then went on to say how she had travelled 2,000 miles to see the race and how her neighbour had been his midwife when he was born. Jimmy muttered something like 'highly unlikely' but she wouldn't be put off. However, Jimmy got a bit fed up with this and she went away.

"A few moments later she came back again to say she had this midwife on the telephone, long distance, and the woman wanted to talk to him. So Jimmy was nailed, there was nothing he could do but go and pick up the telephone and talk to this woman – on race morning! The woman had a Scottish accent and she had been a midwife in Kelso; but of course Jimmy wasn't born in Kelso but in Fife and so he had to explain to her she was mistaken. That he was so patient with her was because she was actually Scottish and had probably been confused, but imagine having to go through that treatment at the very moment when so much was at stake.

"A lot has been said about Hockenheim and his last race and it is not for me to say what went wrong. I don't think the race was important for either Clark or Lotus, for at that time a new Formula 2 car was being prepared at the factory. Indeed they were short-staffed on mechanics because the rest were back at the factory working on the new cars which he hoped to drive at Pau. Jimmy was going to test the new car the day after the German race so I don't think that he was caring very much one way or the other at Hockenheim.

"Later a lot was written in the Press as to why he was there instead of racing the new Ford prototype at Brands Hatch. He had been approached towards the end of 1967 by Alan Mann to see whether he would drive the Ford and he agreed to do so. But at that time Alan hadn't made up the programme of races, and I believe it was left that Alan would let Jimmy know which races he was to drive. Jimmy didn't want to do Le Mans even though at one stage it was on the programme. He had this thing about people whom he felt had crossed him – he would never forget such incidents and one involved the Le Mans organisers. He never forgave them for banning the Lotus 23 in 1962, and swore he wouldn't go back (he didn't like the race anyway, but the 1962 Lotus ban was the last straw). '

"It was left that Alan would write to Jimmy and give him the list of fixtures but I believe that this didn't happen, and there was a last minute rush in March just prior to the introduction of the Ford prototype when Alan Mann's secretary was trying to get a hold of Jimmy. Obviously they wanted him to confirm that he would drive one at Brands Hatch in the B.O.A.C. 500 and to get his O.K. so that they could announce this to the press. Unfortunately, by that time Jimmy had made his plans for the Formula 2 races and had agreed that Andrew Ferguson of Lotus should enter him for Hockenheim on the same weekend. Obviously he was upset that this mix-up had taken place and I am sure that something would have been sorted out for the other races during the season, but, being as stubborn as he was, Jimmy insisted that he had pledged to go to Hockenheim so he went there. As far as I knew it this was the background to his appearance there.

"Jimmy Clark was popular because he was a great man, and at the same time was approachable. In my opinion he was the best driver of his time, and possibly the best of all times. His reactions were quite astonishingly fast – a minor thing which brought this home to me was the fact that he was the only person who could move fast enough completely to outwit my basset hound Lotus in parlour games.

"The real proof of this is to be found, however, in his long racing career. He had only one shunt which was serious, in which he was injured. This, alas, was the final one. Normally, when his car should have been out of control, in a spin for example, Jimmy retained control

Jim Clark

better than anyone else could have in similar circumstances, simply because of his extremely fast reactions and sense of balance. At Indianapolis, for example, he achieved more than once the impossible – spinning and carrying on without touching the wall or stalling his engine. This was an unprecedented feat.

"Over many seasons we always saw him drive so brilliantly, and get away from so many shunts, that we thought that nothing would ever happen to him. Unfortunately, we forgot the part which luck has to play. Jim Clark didn't run out of skill, he ran out of luck."

A Home from Home?
– Bill Bryce and Eoin Young

To an international racing driver the world is his parish. Everywhere enthusiasts want to see what the best driver in the world has to offer, and so, early in his international career, Jim Clark discovered New Zealand and Australia. I remember on his first trip there in 1961 he bubbled over about these countries, and in the following years he was to fit the Tasman series of races into his programme whenever possible. His last Tasman winter was possibly his most successful as, against good opposition, he won the Championship for the third time.

When he spoke of New Zealand and Australia he always had a sparkle in his eye and there was the hint that far away from Britain and Europe he really let his hair down and genuinely enjoyed the country. We used to talk about Australia and New Zealand and, of the two, he probably preferred New Zealand, for the people and the country were so like his native Scotland.

Two journalists and broadcasters who were with Jimmy on his trips down under were Eoin Young and Bill Bryce, both of whom spend their summers in Europe. Their story of Jimmy was a more relaxed one of the side of Jimmy which few people saw, the fun-loving Jim Clark.

For Eoin Young his first meeting with Clark was rather startling. It was at Christchurch during the Lady

Jim Clark

Wigram Trophy meeting, which in 1961 was held in a seemingly perpetual downpour.

"You wouldn't have believed rain like this, it just bucketed down all afternoon and the whole place was ankle deep in mud. The circuit is so flat that it had big puddles all over it. This, remember, was back in the days before people talked about their tyres aquaplaning and they were simply sliding about all over the place. I was walking down the infield parallel with the main straight—it was raining so hard you could barely make out the top of the straight – watching this thing coming towards us throwing up great big clouds of spray. It finally came to a stop about 50 yards from us and turned out to be Jimmy in the Lotus. He had stalled the car. He waved to us and indicated he wanted a push start, so we got behind and pushed like hell, but his tyres could find no grip at all. We just said forget it, but he wasn't having that and wanted us to get the car over on to the track and push it there. We took one look at the other people in the race spinning all over the place and more emphatically said forget it so he got out, shrugged his shoulders and introduced himself to us."

For Bill Bryce the first meeting was rather different.

"I remember chasing him and Innes Ireland down the road from Ardmore in Triumph Heralds we had borrowed – we were having a great old dice. When we got out of the cars Jimmy, by the way I chased after him, thought that I was the owner of the Herald he was driving. He and Innes

134

had pretty guilty consciences about giving the car such a stoning.

"What I liked about Jim was that any time you wanted to speak to him he would be on. I remember at Invercargill interviewing him on radio. He was wandering about and I just said to him how about coming up and talking about racing? So he talked about saloon car racing and we had a great old chat over the national radio in New Zealand. This sort of informality went over so well. He just seemed to relax so much over there in particular. In 1968 for instance, although never keen on functions, he was very anxious to get down to Palmerston North for the Lord Mayor's procession because they had a whole lot of vintage cars in a grand parade which they drove round the streets so that people could see the drivers at lunchtime.

"The night he won the Tasman Cup in 1967 we were doing radio reports back to New Zealand from Australia, and we missed the radio link which operated from Sandown Park in Melbourne. There was frivolity all around and people were drinking champagne by the boot load, so we grabbed Jimmy and did the programme by long-distance telephone – the funniest thing you have ever seen as everyone was getting stoned up to the eyeballs all around us while we recorded this programme.

"I spent a fortnight with him in the Paris flat last year and we had a great deal of fun – such as the time we threw all our clothes into the washing machine and they came out grey because the oil in his overalls had gone through every one of our shirts. These are some of the amusing things you remember about him.

"Maybe it was the atmosphere in New Zealand but after all the races there was a great shebang and though Jimmy didn't drink very much he always joined in the spirit of the thing. Whenever we had a Maori 'war canoe' he would always be one of the first on to the floor and his speeches there were really good, though we know how terrible his speeches could be, and how nervous he was in making them. There was also the time he found a packet of cigarettes in a tent, gathered a bunch of boy scouts around him and gave them the cigarettes. He then had a picture taken of all these boy scouts lined up like a cricket team smoking cigarettes with Jimmy in the middle holding half a gallon of beer.

"At Teratonga this year everyone had a wild time, especially Jimmy because he had just walked away from a big shunt when he went off the road and through a fence but still came back and finished second. He was very relieved after this and there was a real old party going on. He took off to the toilet, a ramshackle affair in corrugated iron; Paul Fahey, the New Zealand saloon car champion, saw him go in there so he raced out and got in his Chevrolet Impala with the Mustang on the trailer in the back and charged the toilet. Just as he leaned the Mustang and trailer on the toilet Jimmy walked out of the door as the whole place collapsed behind him. We also had a do at Invercargill after the 1968 race when someone had given Pedro Rodriguez a bottle of Tequila —we all got into this and Clarkie was on the best form we've ever seen him.

"One of the funniest things about Jimmy was his faith. We were sitting in an aeroplane waiting to fly down from

Wellington to Christchurch with Chris Amon when it was blowing an 80 m.p.h. gale along the tarmac and the wings were leaping up and down on the Viscount. There were about six blokes holding on to each wheel while everyone got on. Amon was over in a corner looking worried, as was everybody; but Clarkie just mutters 'Oh well' and proceeds to fall asleep before the plane even took off. He seemed to be able to relax in situations like this – and leaving Wellington airport in even a 20 m.p.h. gale is a rare old ride!

"The night before we had been up in the hills above Wellington having dinner with some friends and the wind was howling around. We were eating by candlelight and Jimmy was telling us about the ghost at his farm at Edington Mains. We thought he was having us on but he was so sincere about it that we soon realized that he really had seen this ghost. He was talking about the ghost of the Grey Lady which he said he had seen when he was about nine years old. He had thought it was his mother and had apparently said to her something about coming in and seeing him that night and she said she hadn't been near him. He was so sincere that it was one of the eeriest of sensations.

"When Jackie Stewart started coming out for the Tasman races they used to go around together and Jackie, an outgoing type, would tend to make Jimmy the fall guy in his jokes. Jimmy loved this – he never worried about it. But he always used to get his own back on Jackie. There was the feeling that Jimmy was quite happy to let Jackie have his fun, then he would go out and beat him. Together they were very funny people. On another party occasion someone brought a piper down. He arrived when most people were beyond caring, but Stewart and Clark leapt up and they went into a spontaneous wild highland reel which ended when one let go of the other and they both ended up in the flower beds, and Jackie twisted his ankle.

"On a completely different front, when most drivers are faced with another driver's accident they tend not to show any emotion or let it affect their nerves, but Jimmy always seemed to be upset and it appeared to prey on his mind. On the occasion when Donald Campbell was killed I woke him up in a motel and handed him the paper. He just took it and said he would see us later; we didn't see him for a couple of hours although normally we all had breakfast together. He had a way of screwing his face up when something really worried him. Even when some of the local New Zealand drivers had accidents it appeared to affect him and he was very concerned about Denny Hulme's crash in the Tasman Series. At the same time Chris Amon reckoned that Jimmy was very brave, particularly when going in and out of race traffic.

"Another point about him was his approachability. At least we found this. As journalists you have to get around everyone and talk to them, but Jimmy would start a conversation with you and ask all sorts of questions. For a person of his standing to make the running, so to speak, was a big thing. Mind you, again, he would get very odd if someone asked him something stupid. One time at the Nürburgring in the Firestone caravan some little fellow from New York rushed up and said he would like to interview him and Clark said that suited him. The first thing this fellow said was 'How do you like being Graham Hill's team mate?' As quick as a flash he came back 'I'm not Graham Hill's team mate, he's my team mate.' This sort of reply was strange for Jimmy but the whole interview was dead from then on.

"With Jimmy you sometimes got into some odd situations such as when we spent the evening with a chap who invited us to go with him collecting deer carcases up in the west coast mountains on the South Island of New Zealand. We got up at 5.0 in the morning for the flight right into the middle of nowhere. It was totally inaccessible by car and the only way to get there other than by light plane was by pack horse. We flew in and out of the mountains in this little plane with Jimmy sitting beside the pilot until he dropped us down on an airstrip where you could not even have driven a tractor. We loaded the deer carcases, and then we spent about an hour or so with the pilot ferrying them back to the mainroad and then coming back for more. If the guy hadn't come back for us it would have taken a fortnight to reach civilisation. Afterwards we flew around these mountains and up the valleys chasing deer – one flutter from the engine and we would have been in trouble. However, when one was with Jimmy, one had the feeling nothing was going to happen. He wasn't terribly worried and said that there was always a way out of trouble if it happened. He had tremendous confidence in the pilot. He used to calculate things and if he had confidence in someone he wouldn't worry about it.

"The things we will remember about Jimmy are the good times in New Zealand – such as the occasion when we were driving down through the South Island with Jackie Stewart and Jimmy. We stopped at a little service station, out in the wilds on its own. At the time Dunlop had put out a big poster, with a giant portrait of Jim Clark, and there it was staring at us from the service station window. Jimmy got out of the Zephyr and ordered the petrol and Jackie stated to the proprietor, who was serving us, 'that's him there, that's Jim Clark.' The fellow looked at Jimmy, and then this giant portrait right behind him, and he just wouldn't believe it. On the other hand we later called into a shop in the middle of nowhere and bought milk shakes. Afterwards it took us a quarter of an hour to get away, as the whole population of the little village gathered around to collect Jimmy's autograph. He reacted to these contrasting situations with equal good humour.

"At the Lady Wigram Trophy this year Jimmy saw one of the mechanics painting a kiwi on the side of the Gold Leaf Team Lotus car, which was making its first appearance in its new colours. He decided he would go and get a thistle or a St. Andrews flag to add to this, so he grabbed a car and went up into Christchurch to try and get a flag in the souvenir shops but in the end he couldn't get one.

"Then, at a party at a beach house owned by a friend, a lot of drivers, including Jackie Stewart, went out in rowing boats. Jimmy jumped into a speedboat and started doing the Spanish Armada bit in and out of the other boats. This led to a lot of splashing about with oars and finally Jackie was left with no oars about 300 yards from the shore. Jimmy told him to throw a line, but instead of towing him into shore, he pulled him farther out into the lake, then gave him back his oars and left him there...

"New Zealand and Australia seemed to appeal to his 'out-door' instincts and he tended to be very uninhibited out there – he could go water ski-ing or boating or do anything else he wanted to do, more or less when he wanted to. He was a 'bloke', and regarded as one by the people in New Zealand and Australia."

A Gentle Guiding Hand
– Walter Hayes

Motor racing has been called madness and it has also been called a branch of show business – certainly, no matter what personal views may be held on this pursuit, one cannot overlook the fact that commercialism envelopes it today. I am among those who welcome commercialism for, whereas it has destroyed a number of things, I don't think it has destroyed motor racing; it has enriched it. It has eroded the class system which existed in motor racing before the war and shortly afterwards and it has given a sharper and more competitive edge to the sport. The days of Brooklands may have been idyllic for members of that generation but today the values are different and the people in motor racing are different. Some may criticise the way in which money is apparently thrown around in motor racing, but without the money the cars we have today would not exist and the sport would be no more honest. It is a reasonably fair sport where, in the end, it is still a battle between man and man, machine and machine; the former to satisfy natural ego and the latter to satisfy the need for progress.

Today a man can become a racing driver much more easily than a few years ago, particularly in Britain which is well endowed with circuits and a heavy programme of races. He will still have to have some money, although in relative terms it need not be a great amount; he does have to have ability and the general standard of competition in the rough and tumble of club racing today is much higher than in the early post-war years. That there are better cars to drive is obvious, but I recall Jimmy Clark remarking that, in Europe in particular, the trend has been towards developing drivers who are not only quick but tidy. After all, if a rising contender wants to get anywhere in motor racing today he has to keep up with the mob and at the same time stay on the island for, in order to get the next step up on the ladder, potential sponsors must be assured that he is not going to break motor cars in so doing. This is a situation which does not exist to the same degree in the U.S. where motor sport offers fewer factory drives and there is a greater premium on spectacle.

As the sport develops so does the cost of administering it and paying for it, so through the years a solid wedge of sponsors have come along and added their contribution to the development of the sport. In recent years no company has added more with greater effect than Ford Motor Company, and in Britain the man mainly responsible for the upsurge in interest by that company has been Walter Hayes, who today is Director of Public Affairs for Ford Europe.

A brilliant and successful man at his craft, Hayes has become an internationally known figure in motor racing, a man as respected for his judgement as his cars are respected for their performance. It was he who pushed forward the idea that Ford should be committed to racing and rallying and in doing so he was breaking with the Ford past, so to speak. He felt in the early 'sixties that the time was ripe to foster the sport and for Ford to do themselves what others had been doing anyway with their engines. (I believe one design engineer at Ford, responsible for the development of the 105E engine, remarked, on seeing the tremendous power outputs some tuners were getting from the engine, that he must have made a lousy job of over-engineering it in the first place. Of course when it was first produced no one at Ford ever dreamed of the lengths to which the 105E and its derivatives would be developed, but the ingredients were there, just needing to be stirred.)

When the decision was taken to go into motor racing, money was diverted to the most likely sources of success – to Colin Chapman at Lotus and to Mike Costin and Keith Duckworth at Cosworth, and later to Alan Mann. The outcome was the decision by Ford to build a Grand Prix engine, something which would have been unthinkable to the late Henry Ford and probably unimaginable to the Board of Ford Motor Company before Walter Hayes came along. But Hayes stuck his neck out even further and gambled, literally, his own reputation as well as his job on this giant commitment—and it has paid off. Today, Ford sales around the world are leaping ahead and their competition successes have played a big part in making the name mean something different.

For Hayes the development of the Formula I engine was a timely intervention at a period when Coventry Climax had withdrawn from racing, leaving the responsibility of building British engines with B.R.M. By bringing out the Ford engine he relieved the pressure on

B.R.M. and, at the same time, brought something new into Grand Prix racing just when it needed a change of scenery.

Walter Hayes is a man of medium height who exudes style. He dresses well, smokes a pipe and has a soft well-modulated voice which goes with his "Father Figure" image amongst the racing set. For him Jim Clark meant two things: firstly, he was an important cog in the Ford wheel through his link with Colin Chapman and Lotus, and secondly, he was someone whom Hayes felt needed protection from some of the harsh business realities of life.

"I made the point in a short obituary I wrote for *Ford Times* that other people drove motor cars but Jim Clark was able to show what a motor car was capable of. And there is quite a phenomenal difference between the two types. In all his conversation he would never say what he could do or what he thought, he would always talk about the car and what the car could do. Some drivers drive as though they have to dominate the machinery but I think Jimmy drove like a ballet dancer, he had the lightest feet and hands on earth. He had immensely strong shoulders and arms but this was the only part of him that was strong physically. He was a great dancer in motor cars, gentle with them, kind with them and I feel that the reason he was a great driver was that there was always the feeling of participation with the motor car, so the driving almost became sixth sense with him in many cases. At Nürburgring I once dumped my eleven-year-old son into the back seat of a Cortina Lotus when Jimmy was going off round the 'Ring. Now, I wouldn't let this little boy passenger with racing drivers because he is precious to me, but you would let anybody drive with Jimmy.

"I never knew anyone to say anything nasty about Jimmy. I know this is the kind of thing you get after someone has been killed, an obituary insincerity, but people didn't say horrid things about· him because he never did anything horrid.

"I think there is an image of Clark that one must try and bury and that is this thing about Jimmy and the sheep. The reason Jimmy would go back to the farm was because his family was there – and it isn't a sheep farm anyway, it is an arable farm. I think he liked going back to it in the earlier days, but I think later he went only to see the family for I don't think he cared very much about the sheep. All this stuff about Jimmy the shepherd with his little flat cap was nonsense. He wasn't a great shepherd. He liked to go back to the family every so often to rediscover who he was.

"I am not suggesting that Jimmy wasn't interested in farming, but the public version of Jimmy going back to tend the sheep was a long way from being true. The background to the family had also got more than a little twisted for they were not the Highland shepherds some people have suggested they were. One of the most invigorating things to my mind in the weeks following Jimmy's death was the unbelievable strength of his father, a fabulous character by any standards.

"It was probably late in 1962 that I first came into contact with Jim Clark when the Cortina was coming along and we were about to think intelligently about going further into the competition business. I had known

Colin Chapman for a good many years and indeed when I used to edit the *Sunday Dispatch* and he had his small garage up in Hornsey, I had hired him as motoring correspondent. He was an unknown sort of boy at that time, but obviously a bright up-and-comer.

"When we decided to come into closer touch with the sport we decided that one of the things we would do would be to go into motor racing with Lotus, and so I had a part to play in bringing Lotus and Ford together with things like the Lotus Cortina. When we decided to do a proper racing programme it seemed natural we should talk about drivers and then of course came the first meeting I had with Jim Clark. Even then I had the feeling there were a number of people who didn't know too much about him. He had a comparatively brief time at the absolute top and from then on we had a friendly-cum-business-cum-advisory sort of relationship which lasted right up to the very last minute. The arrangement we always had was that we had a contract with Colin Chapman and a separate contract with Jim Clark because there were a number of things we wanted him to do for us which had nothing really to do with Lotus. He did a lot of testing and the occasional rally. He was very interested in helping the motor industry and he used to do a tremendous amount of ambassadorial work for us overseas. The number of places where the Cortina was introduced to the public by Jim Clark was quite exceptional. On one occasion he agreed we would do a Scandinavian tour which required travelling to Sweden, Norway and Denmark and it was all laid on. His father's back had been bothering him so Jimmy insisted that he go home to see his father and I sent a private Dove aircraft to Edinburgh to pick him up and fly him to Stockholm, which is a terrible journey in a Dove. I met him in the early morning and we then did all the various trips, finally arriving in Denmark. The Danish press were so enthusiastic that when we flew out to go to Holland the airline held up the plane while he gave a press conference. Then for the first time I saw Jim Clark's magic at work. When we were in Holland and went into a night club things were getting tedious and boring until I noticed this beautiful hostess at the bar. I went over to talk to her and she asked me if I would do something for her. I said anything, and she asked if I would get her Jim Clark's autograph. I decided that night that when a little hostess in a Dutch night club could recognise on sight this little man and crave for his autograph he must be a great man, and he gave her the autograph with a certain amount of pleasure.

"When I first met Jimmy he found it extremely difficult to speak in public and he was exceptionally shy about it. In the last years of his life he was really very good, not as good as Graham Hill but good all the same. The great and extraordinary thing about him was this sincerity which seemed to come over. He could say things and people knew he was telling the truth, because he was so patently sincere in what he was saying. You could never get him to say anything he didn't really believe. There was no question of this, and one would have been insane to try to dictate what he said, so although he used to ask us what he should say about the car we used to tell him to say what he liked about it. He was endlessly willing to drive people around circuits, talk about cars and discuss cars and he was always very interested. He really was a tremendous ambassador for us overseas.

"In the early days you could look at him and he wasn't so well dressed as he became when he was an International personality, nor was he as suave or worldly as he became. Later his suits improved and so many things about him changed. In those early days he was a tremendously simple young man and this was the awe-inspiring thing about him. I used to stand and look at him endlessly and ask myself 'what is it, how is it possible?'

"My wife has a theory that there are only two racing drivers who look like racing drivers – Jo Bonnier and Graham Hill. She doesn't think that any of the others look like racing drivers. She thought Jimmy was very handsome but somehow he didn't look as a racing driver should look, and I must say in the early days I would have agreed about that.

"He was terribly un-businesslike. To my knowledge September had arrived one year not so long ago and there were still no signed contracts with anyone. Where we were concerned we would tell him what we would like him to do and he would tell us what he wouldn't do, and we would then agree how much we thought we ought to pay him. Then we would say 'fine' and it was never referred to again, never mentioned. I used to have in the early days a slight suspicion that he wouldn't really argue for money and he never ever asked us for more than we offered. One became very protective and felt one had to take care of this young man because he didn't know how to ask for more. There was one occasion when he rang me up and asked me if I could meet him in London and he said that he had never really thought about money – and this I swear was after he was World Champion – but now he was in a difficult situation for he was getting into the bigger time and could I advise him as to how much he should ask people? He emphasised it had to be on a reasonable basis because he didn't want to be greedy and yet at the same time he didn't want to let the other drivers down. I don't believe he ever had the first idea of his market value until the last two years of his life. Now I know this isn't the popular belief, and it isn't what people say, but the first year Clark drove for us we paid him £1500. We paid him this because I didn't know any better and he didn't know any better. When I said to him half way through the season 'I don't think it's enough', he replied 'why not?'

"This certainly isn't the popular impression of Clark, who is supposed to have made a great deal of money. I think he did know what it was all about fairly recently because along came Jackie Stewart. Jackie was the great catalyst in money and he has been more instrumental in jacking up racing drivers' fees than any other man in the business. The so-called fabulous sums of money Jimmy was supposed to be getting he never really did get until the last two or three years. The point I am trying to make is how un-worldly wise he was even when you would have expected it not to be so. Take the other top racing drivers of the day – I don't think any of them have this sort of un-businesslike approach.

"A man is influenced by his surroundings and you find you can afford things you never thought possible. At Watkins Glen last year we had dinner in a tent in the garden of Cameron Artensinger (who runs the American Grand Prix). The table consisted of Colin Chapman, Graham Hill, Jim Clark and Denny Hulme and I was the only man at that table who didn't have his own aeroplane. A considerable amount of the conversation was concerned with landing in here and what radio aids you need there and lurid descriptions of Graham Hill landing at Stranraer. So there we were sitting at the party on the evening of the United States Grand Prix and I had to ask if they minded changing the conversation as I felt out of it all. And they said 'Oh you've got to have your own aeroplane' and they were talking about it not like *nouveaux riches*, but like people to whom a private aeroplane had become indispensible.

"You may not care about International restaurants and the finest menus in the world but after a while you stop thinking 'here I am in a famous restaurant'; it comes quite naturally to you. Your tailoring becomes better not because you have consciously thought that your tailoring should become better but because it becomes quite natural to go and buy your clothes from a famous tailor. What had happened to Clark was that familiarity with this kind of world in which he lived rubbed off on him in a way that I think just changed his outward appearance but not himself, not at all.

"He was also a very honest racing man and I have never told this story before – to my mind it is an extraordinary Jim Clark story. We signed Graham and

Jimmy for the Lotus Ford team in 1967 because we particularly wanted to have two good drivers running in the team together. I told Jimmy we were thinking of hiring Graham and asked if it would upset him in any way. He replied that it would not, for he and Graham were old friends.

"The Press was full of the stories of who was the number one and who was the number two in the team, but this was something we never discussed and never felt that it needed discussion. I don't think there was any question but that they should both drive as individuals and if need be should be allowed to race against each other. However, there was one exception during the season and that was the American Grand Prix at Watkins Glen. The night before the race Jimmy, Colin, Graham and I gathered in Graham's bedroom and I said that I felt this was a race vitally important to all of us and, though I hadn't said it before, I would like to run it under a little discipline. I asked them how they would like to run the race and Colin said we could toss a coin to see who would come first and who would come second – we were very confident. Both agreed they didn't mind. We tossed a coin, Graham called, Graham won and it was decided that Graham would be first and Jimmy would be second. I again asked if anyone was worried about this and they said 'no'. If a decision had to be made this is how they would finish. Then in the race, when Graham was leading Jimmy a few laps from the end, he lost a gear and it looked as if he was in real trouble for he dropped right back. Jimmy came past the pits and put both hands up in the air shrugging his shoulders, knowing he had taken the lead and wondering what should he do. Chapman said 'what should we do?' and I said we had no alternative. So we put out the 'Go' and waved our fists at him and he went. Then Graham, though he had apparently lost a gear, suddenly began to motor very fast and catch up again, but we had no time then to start playing games, so the race in fact finished the opposite way to that we had planned.

"The first thing which Jimmy did when he got out of the motor car was to rush back to Graham and say, 'they told me to and I hope you don't mind'. Graham said, 'I know what happened, mate, everything's fine'. It is quite extraordinary that the first thing Jimmy should do is go back to Graham and say he was driving under instruction. This, incidentally, is the only time the question of priorities ever came up, for it was the one race where we had reached the high peak of confidence where we knew we were going to have a one-two because the cars and engines were going so well.

"Jimmy's attitude to life and racing in America was quite different, because until he started to become very famous in the world, he really didn't know very much about the world, and it is a fact that a lot of racing drivers in their early years take a long time to learn about it. You can go to race meeting after race meeting but you haven't been to America. You haven't been to Belgium, you have just been to Zolder. You go in and out and you don't really get to know anything about these places. It wasn't until later on, when he began to get more leisure and his extraordinary racing programme was reduced, when he began to live abroad, that he began to understand overseas people in the way he understood the British.

"The difficulty he had in understanding the States was that success is quite different there to what it is over here. People in this country rush up and congratulate a guy who finishes eighth, but in America it is much more important to come first. It is also much more worthwhile to come first because the prize money is greater and the commercial value is greater. I think Jimmy found the cut-and-thrust in America rather unfamiliar to him. Some of it he didn't care for very much. Whereas a chap in this country with £300 at stake for a win in a race can be pretty hail-fellow-well-met, even an Englishman doesn't become quite so relaxed when he has 120,000 dollars sitting at the end of it, and I think he found there was this greater degree of competitiveness about America. He wasn't any different to the people in America he got on well with. Most people just called him a nice little guy. When he went to the Ford head-quarters in Dearborn after gaining second place at Indianapolis in 1963, they sent the company 'plane to fetch him and he had lunch with the top brass. The top brass in Ford were not familiar with racing drivers as such and they were fairly sophisticated international men who had been around all the time, but I think they were just charmed by him. I swear you could have deposited Clark on a desert island with a bunch of cannibals and in two weeks they would write you a letter to tell you what a nice chap he was.

"I once heard him raise his voice and that was when an autograph hunter came into the garage at the Nürburgring when a technical problem was being discussed, but later on he would have signed all the autographs anyone wanted. If there was one group of people that he didn't like it was newspapermen. He didn't like them as a bunch, although he liked some of them individually, and the reason he didn't like them was that, whereas he was willing to talk all night about motor racing, too many of them wanted to talk about death and girl friends. I have been interested in this point about talking to a racing driver about death and fear, because a racing driver doesn't really think about it. People imagine that drivers think about death but they never do. They know when they have been frightened and they frighten themselves every race, even Jimmy. But I frighten myself going down the Kingston Bypass and I don't expect that much to happen. Jimmy hated people talking to him about death because he didn't know what to say, he didn't have an answer. It was no good saying he never thought about it because it would sound insincere but, as a matter of fact, he never did think about it. This is why I think he felt the journalists were not really interested in asking him the questions he wanted to answer.

"Those who asked him the questions he wanted to answer got some surprisingly intelligent replies. You could say things to him about racing tyres being too big to be sensible, or ask why monocoques are better than space frames, or ask about handling and he would discuss things like the mechanics of drift. He wasn't the great engineering driver, a Richie Ginther or Bruce McLaren *par excellence*. He couldn't define in the early days what was wrong with the car and this irritated him. He would come back and say it was twitchy on a corner but he wasn't precise, so he worked until he did become a good test driver and did begin to learn what it was all about.

"I think there was another fundamental thing about Clark: I do not believe that he ever had a lesson in anything. I don't believe anyone ever taught him anything and I believe that anything he did he worked out for himself. I believe that, in so far as there was a natural genius who developed into a self-made man as far as motor racing was concerned, this was Clark. He would discuss and argue with Chapman but would never do anything or try anything until he had convinced himself it was the right thing to do. He had implicit faith in Colin Chapman and Chapman's relationship with Clark was as rewarding to Clark as it was to Chapman. For example, when we put the Lotus Ford into the Dutch Grand Prix in 1967 it was the first time it had appeared on the track and Jimmy had never even seen the car until it got to Zandvoort. He leaped straight into it and set off to beat the lap record in about three laps. Then he would come back and talk about what the car was doing, but his faith was quite extraordinary, and of course it was repaid because Chapman would do anything for him. This is one of the unfortunate things which has remained. People talk to me about Chapman's suspensions breaking but, compare what has happened to other people— when it is scrutinised Chapman's record is no worse than anyone else's. People tend to forget how much he has done.

"On the personal side, Jimmy would never voluntarily be thrust into crowds. He knew what having a laurel wreath round your neck meant – the obligations that come with it – and he was aware of the crowds. He would drive the Lotus Cortinas conscious of the crowd, and would say so and he loved it, but he remained an excessively shy person right to the very end of his life, although he got more sophisticated as time went by. If you go to France and you can't speak French and then go to France when you can speak French, you find France an entirely different country. I think this is what happened to Jim Clark. He started out unable to talk the language of international living. Then he found he could speak the language and suddenly things changed for him, not because he was any different, but because he had learned the language.

"His greatest advantage, I think, was that he knew who he was. He was entirely at ease with his circumstances and I think this was very important for he didn't have to go along trying to prove anything to anyone. He had a great basic security right from the beginning. People remarked he bit his nails. I bite my nails, but I don't think it proves anything. I have seen him tense, but I have never seen him tense about motor racing. I feel you can always tell happy people because happy people never know what they are going to do tomorrow. This may seem a rather stupid definition, but if in 1965 you asked Jimmy what he was going to do in 1966 he didn't know and he couldn't tell you because he wasn't really willing to think about it. He wanted to think about today and tomorrow. I don't think he ever in the whole of his life said 'next year I will . . .' until he was so near to next year he had to. All his life he just lived a year at a time. This is one of the reasons why he didn't marry and settle down, because he had great friendships and very good friends and marriage was something it was possible to think about when he was in the mood to think about next year but he hadn't yet reached that moment.

"I think I shall miss a number of things in the 1968 season. The first is that Jimmy never asked for anything. Motor racing is a demanding business, people are always coming to you with ideas and problems but Jimmy is the one I particularly recall in this respect, because he never caused me any trouble. That I shall always regard with a great deal of affection. I shall also miss the quiet before or after race lunches and dinners when I had him to myself and could get him just to talk in a way you could only rarely get him to talk – just about motor racing. He was terribly good at it. The third thing, which I think everyone is going to miss, is practice, and that incredible electric moment when you saw him get into the car and the question would be 'what's Jimmy going to do?'. He was always going to do something a little better than everybody else and there was this thing of seeing him come back after setting up lap times which just didn't seem feasible.

"I cannot divorce myself from the racing-on-the-track man – that was the electric Clark – yet there was always this thing about feeling protective towards him, that you had to take care of him."

The Perfect Partnership
– Colin Chapman

"The first I ever heard of Jim Clark was from Jock McBain, who had been purchasing Lotus sports cars from us for two or three years. He mentioned this young farmer, already legendary up in the Borders, whom he felt was a very, very good driver. One of the first occasions I really met Jimmy was when he came down to Brands Hatch to try out a Formula 2 car, on behalf of Border Reivers, who were thinking of purchasing one. There and then I was most impressed with the way he drove the car, especially as it was his first single-seater drive, and also his first drive at Brands Hatch. He was steady, consistent and, basically, just downright competent. At around about the same time, he drove a Lotus Elite for the Border Reivers at Le Mans, doing very well indeed, and my impression of his performance then was reinforced when he drove at Brands Hatch one Boxing Day in an Elite.

"I drove in that same race, and we had quite a dice together. Immediately afterwards I asked him if he would like to join Team Lotus. This was during the period when Team Lotus was in a stage of transition, from being a racing team in which I was the principal driver, and thus was virtually being run for my benefit, to the point where I was sponsoring a team for other drivers.

This transition therefore coincided with Jimmy coming to Lotus and therefore he was the first driver to actually come to the team as its principal driver. So really we came of age together: Lotus was just getting into Grand Prix racing, Jimmy was just getting into Grand Prix racing. The fact therefore that we were both learning together made our association very interesting, and so very fruitful.

"As far as I was concerned, I felt right from the beginning that he was such a good driver, and a man with whom I was so completely at one, that I could retire from driving myself and concentrate purely on producing cars for Jimmy to drive. And this is in fact what I did. We always got on so terribly well – we thought alike and acted alike, we were both keen on doing a thoroughly first class job, and we found out about racing together. This is something which will never ever be the same again for me in motor racing, because of all the problems, all the successes and the anguish we shared together (and there's a lot of anguish in motor racing). Throughout it all Jimmy realised we were both finding our feet and was very friendly, very co-operative. For me, this made it enjoyable, easy and pleasant.

"As we went along, too, he developed a superb technical knowledge. When he started driving for me, he didn't of course have the benefit of a formal engineering background. But he did have what I can only describe as a very very good intellect, and he picked up the engineering side of motor racing so rapidly that after a while I was able to interpret his expressions regarding the car, its handling and its requirements and so on.

The power comes out here—contemplating the Ford V-8 and
the transmission of the Lotus 49

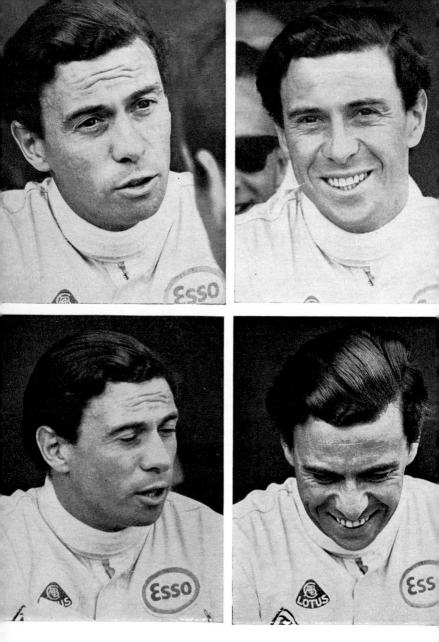

Jimmy chatti

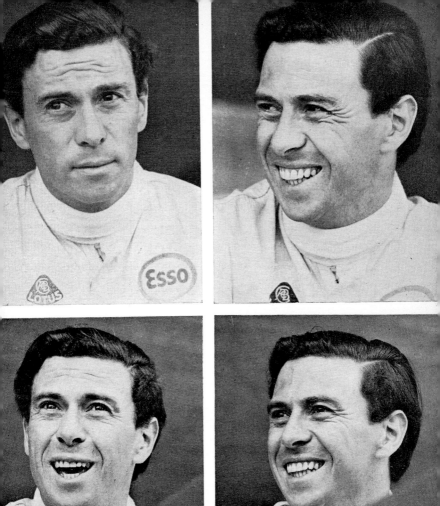

the pits at Watkins Glen, 1967)

Between-races fun in New Zealand's Lake Taupo

And this made it easier for me to develop better motor cars.

"Although at first certainly, he wasn't a development driver in the accepted sense I think I got even better results than I might have with a driver trained in the engineering sense. For Jimmy had no real preconceived ideas, he was merely satisfied with reporting the facts, what actually happened, and did not try to draw his own conclusions. And of course, in many ways, this is an ideal driver for an engineer to work with – unfortunately, you do find that some drivers who have some little engineering knowledge will form their own conclusions about what is happening, and, possibly subconsciously, make the facts fit their conclusions. This Jimmy never did.

"I think the thing about Jimmy Clark as a driver was that he was relaxed, he was always in command of the situation and he very very rarely drove beyond nine tenths of his capacity. The result was that he always appeared to be smooth and extremely competent. He had so much natural ability that he was driving within himself far more than most drivers do.

"There were occasions when he drove really hard and of course those were the rare occasions when he showed his sheer genius for being able to drive so much quicker than any other contemporary driver. I remember that 1962 German Grand Prix at Nürburgring, when on the start line he forgot to switch his fuel pumps on, and so was left behind at the start. This was the sort of thing that would raise the tiger in him, because he felt, rightly or wrongly, that he had made a mistake and it was up to him to put it right. He just drove fantastically well that day, so that although he only finished fourth in the motor race I would put this motor race down as one of his best. Similarly, in the Italian Grand Prix at Monza in 1967 he did something which up to that point I, and I think most people, had felt was impossible. He had a puncture which dropped him a lap and a quarter behind, and at Monza he actually made up a lap on the field – even if you do have a capability of going faster than the other drivers, at Monza you invariably end up towing them round with you. But Jimmy actually caught the leaders, left them, and then made up a whole lap on them. This I think was a virtuoso drive which no other driver has ever equalled or will ever be able to surpass.

"This was just one of the rare drives in Jimmy's career when he drove flat out. I can only think of four or five other occasions in the whole ten years he drove for me that he really drew on all his resources. Because generally he was capable of making a very quick start, getting out in front of the opposition, and demoralising them. From that moment on he drove to a plan of his own which conserved the machinery, which conserved his own energies, and was adequate to win the race.

"I never controlled him when he was racing, all I did was give him the maximum amount of information, and let him run the motor race. I believe that the driver is the only man qualified to make the decisions, for example how fast to go; he is the only man who can size up his capability, how much he's extending himself, how much he is extending his car, what the condition of the track is, and so on. I think it is absolutely futile for any team manager as such to try to manage a car during a race. His purpose is to give the driver information; the driver decides on the tactics of the race and drives accordingly.

"I do not think it was true that he was always happiest in a single-seater, or that he ever, ever really played to the crowds. I think, for example, that he used to enjoy Cortina racing just because he enjoyed racing – he got a lot of fun from it. In fact he used to tell me that some of the most enjoyable rides, from his own personal point of view, were when he drove Cortinas, because the car was relatively difficult – it wasn't a precise racing car, it was a car that you could play around with, throw about. He could do all sorts of ridiculous things with it, and he just used to enjoy it – not because it pleased the crowd, but because it pleased him.

"I don't think Jimmy took any notice of the crowd, he certainly was never racing for his public as it were. He was racing for himself.

"I think he enjoyed sports cars, too. In fact he liked to try any different form of racing – this was a thing which evolved through his career. This really is why he went to Indianapolis, certainly he did not go because he believed all the mumbo jumbo that surrounds the race, it was just that it was a new type of motor racing, so he wanted to try it. For the same reason, he later tried an American stock car race, merely because it was something new, and he enjoyed tackling new things. He would get as much fun out of driving even a kart as he would out of driving a racing car. Anything that needed co-ordination and control was exciting to him.

"For the same reason he really loved flying. In fact I remember just before his accident, he was talking about his future and what he was going to do when he stopped racing, and he said he finally made up his mind that he wouldn't in fact go back to farming. He still loved it, but I think he would have found it difficult to go back to it after the excitement and turmoil of racing, flying and the life he had been leading. I think he wanted to settle down in some branch of the aviation business. He certainly had some business investments in aviation in Australia, although I do not think he could have settled down out there, as some people imagined. He certainly enjoyed Australia and New Zealand very much, he enjoyed the climate and he enjoyed the people (Australia I think probably more than New Zealand). While I don't know if he would have gone out there to live, I don't think so; I think he would have probably come back to Europe.

"It is difficult to say of course, how long he might have gone on racing. We had talked about it briefly and I think he would have certainly seen the current Formula out to the end of 1970.

"In his racing one achievement was not fulfilled – he had won every major Grand Prix apart from Monaco, and he would dearly have loved to have won at Monaco. He actively disliked a few circuits–Spa most of all. He felt it was a dangerous circuit, and he was always very happy to get the Belgian Grand Prix over. This could have been due to the fact that the second Grand Prix race he ever did was at Spa when his team mate Alan Stacey met with a fatal accident, and I think this sort of thing made a lasting impression on him. Certainly the season always seemed a lot more relaxed once the Spa race was finished.

"He never used to like Silverstone very much. Not because he felt it was a dangerous circuit, he just felt it was an uninteresting circuit. But, as well as Monaco, he did like Nürburgring – this was another of his favourites, because I think these two were more challenging than most of the others.

"One of the things about Jimmy was that he had the ability to adapt himself, or train himself, to cope with almost any situation in life. This showed in his development as an international figure. When he was World Champion for the first time the speeches and public appearances he had to make were very foreign to him and he had to work very hard at them. But, like anything he tackled, he very quickly mastered this aspect of his career. This was just another problem to him, and within a year he had licked it. If he hadn't have been a first-rate racing driver, I am sure he would have been at the top of what ever profession he went in for.

"I have been thinking very much about Jimmy and racing drivers and trying to analyse what really made him so much better at his business than others and I think it must boil down to that he just had a very very superior intellect. He was very quick to assess a situation, and not necessarily only whilst driving. His mind had the resolving power to be able to sift extraneous material from important matters, and surely this is a mark of anyone who is truly great in any profession, that they can sort the trivial from the essential.

"He also had such exceptional physical attributes, of eyesight, co-ordination and so on. Not only did he have these physical attributes, but he had the mental ability to go with them, plus a tremendous self control which must have stemmed from his family background, his upbringing, and his school. I have met his parents really closely only since his accident, and seeing the way they reacted to it and bore up under the adversity, I realize that this is where he got this fantastic dourness. Farming must have played a part in his moulding, too, for I think that farmers in general must accept life and its quirks to a much greater degree than most people – they have to accept the influence that weather and other things outside their normal control have upon their own lives, and on their prosperity. And possibly too, this showed in the way that Jimmy had an approach which was always resigned to some of the problems of life and living. This capacity made him able to cope with them so exceptionally well.

"Looking round at other racing drivers, now, I think without undue prejudice – although I must admit to a little – I can't see any that have anywhere near the total ability that Jimmy had. Really, his ability was so much greater than even he revealed. As I have said he rarely drove to his capacity, very rarely indeed, and this makes the gulf between him and other racing drivers even bigger. Certainly it is bigger than is shown purely by the record book. It wasn't what he did, it was the way he did it. He did it with such reserves, that it was almost incredible to believe that it was possible to find such reserves in one man.

"I feel that although he was pre-eminent as a racing driver, I do not feel this is the biggest credit to Jim Clark. I think that his most profound influence, certainly on me and all his close associates, was not his ability as a racing driver, but his success as a man. He was so thoroughly adjusted to life and its problems, he had such a thorough integrity of his own that it is very difficult for others to compare themselves in the same street. He was fit, he was honest – 'integrity' is the best single word to describe his qualities. This is the man I shall always remember, not simply a man who won a record number of races. He was a man who set an example to others."

The Record
– Jim Clark's Competition Career

1956

Date and Circuit	Event	Car	Result
June 3			
Stobs Camp Sprint	Saloons over 2,000 cc	Sunbeam Mk 3	1st
June 16			
Crimond	Sports under 1,200 cc	DKW	8th
Sept. 30			
Winfield Sprint	Saloons under 1,200 cc	DKW	1st
	Modified saloons under 1,500 cc	DKW	1st
	Saloons, unlimited	Sunbeam	1st
	Modified saloons, unlimited	Sunbeam	1st
Oct. 7			
Brunton Beadnell	High-Speed Trials	DKW	6th
		Sunbeam	6th

1957

Date and Circuit	Event	Car	Result
June 30			
Charterhall	Production Cars Handicap	DKW	4th
Sept. 1			
Charterhall	Sports 1,501–2,700 cc	Sunbeam Mk 3	8th
Oct. 5			
Charterhall	Production Sports Cars (Handicap)	Porsche 1600S	3rd
	Production Touring Cars (Handicap)	Porsche 1600S	2nd
	BMRC Trophy	Porsche 1600S	1st
Oct. 6			
Winfield Sprint	Modified saloons (unlimited)	Porsche 1600S	1st
	Sports Cars, 1,501–3,000 cc	Porsche 1600S	2nd

1958

Date and Circuit	Event	Car	Result
April 5			
Full Sutton	Racing Cars, over 500 cc	Jaguar D-type	1st
	Sports Cars, unlimited	Jaguar D-type	1st
	Production Sports Cars, unlimited	Porsche 1600S	6th

Date and Circuit	Event	Car	Result
April 20			
Winfield Sprint	Saloons under 2,000 cc	Porsche	1st
	Sports Cars, unlimited	Porsche	2nd
April 27			
Charterhall	Racing, Formule Libre	Jaguar D-type	8th
	Sports Cars, 1,501–3,000 cc	Porsche 1600S	4th
	Sports Cars, under 2,000 cc	Porsche	Ret.
May 18			
Spa-Francorchamps	GP de Spa (over 1,500 cc)	Jaguar D-type	8th
	GT Specials (under 2,000 cc)	Porsche 1600S	5th
May 24			
Full Sutton	Sports Cars, unlimited	Jaguar D-type	1st
	Formule Libre	Jaguar	1st
	Saloon and GT Cars, unlimited	Porsche 1600S	1st
June 8			
Stobs Camp Sprint	Sports Cars, under 2,000 cc	Porsche	1st
	Sports Cars, under 2,000 cc	Triumph TR3	2nd

Date and Circuit	Event	Car	Result
June 21			
Crimond	Sports Cars, unlimited	Jaguar D-type	1st
	Sports Cars, 1,500–3,000 cc	Porsche 1600S	4th
	Invitation Handicap	Jaguar D-type	8th
June 28			
Rest-and-be Thankful Hill Climb	Production Sports Cars, 1,501–2,000 cc	Porsche 1600S	1st
	Production Sports Cars, 1,501–2,000 cc	Triumph TR3	3rd
June 29			
Charterhall	Formule Libre	Jaguar D-type	1st
	Sports Cars, unlimited	Jaguar D-type	1st
July 5			
Rest-and-be-Thankful Hill Climb	Sports Cars, 1,501–2,000 cc	Porsche 1600S	1st
	Sports Cars, 1,501–2,000 cc	Triumph TR3	2nd
July 6			
Charterhall	Racing Cars (Handicap)	Jaguar D-type	1st
	Touring Cars (Handicap)	Porsche 1600S	2nd
	Production Sports Cars (Handicap)	Porsche	4th
	BMRC Trophy (Handicap)	Jaguar D-type	2nd

Date and Circuit	Event	Car	Result
July 12			
Full Sutton	Formule Libre	Jaguar D-type	1st
	Sports Cars, over 1,500 cc	Jaguar D-type	1st
	Sports Cars, under 1,600 cc	Porsche 1600S	1st
July 27			
Winfield Sprint	Touring Cars, modified over 1,500 cc	Porsche	1st
	Sports Cars, 1,501–3,000 cc	Porsche	1st
	Sports-Racing Cars, unlimited	Jaguar D-type	1st
Aug. 4			
Mallory Park	Sports Cars, over 1,500 cc	Jaguar D-type	1st
	Formule Libre Heat	Jaguar D-type	2nd
	Final	Jaguar D-type	7th
Aug. 16			
Silverstone	Six Hour Relay Race (Handicap)	Porsche	22nd
Sept. 28			
Charterhall	Formule Libre	Jaguar D-type	2nd
	Sports Cars, over 1,500 cc	Jaguar D-type	3rd
	Sports Cars, under 1,600 cc	Porsche 1600S	3rd

Date and Circuit	Event	Car	Result
Dec. 26			
Brands Hatch	GT Cars, unlimited	Lotus Elite	2nd

1959

Date and Circuit	Event	Car	Result
March 30			
Mallory Park	GT Cars, 1,000–1,600 cc	Lotus Elite	1st
	Sports Cars, over 1,200 cc	Lister-Jaguar	1st
	Formule Libre, Heat	Lister-Jaguar	1st
	Final	Lister-Jaguar	1st
April 11			
Oulton Park	Sports Cars, under 1,500 cc	Lotus Elite	10th
	Sports Cars, over 1,500 cc	Lister-Jaguar	8th
April 18			
Aintree	Sports Cars, over 1,500 cc	Lister-Jaguar	6th
April 25			
Charterhall	Sports Cars, over 2,000 cc	Lister-Jaguar	1st
	Formule Libre	Lister-Jaguar	1st
	GT Cars, under 1,600 cc	Porsche 1600S	2nd

Date and Circuit	Event	Car	Result
May 18			
Goodwood	Whitsun Trophy (Sports Cars)	Lister-Jaguar	Ret.
May 30			
Rufforth	Sports Cars, unlimited	Lister-Jaguar	1st
	Formule Libre	Lister-Jaguar	2nd
June 7			
Stobs Camp Sprint	GT Cars, under 1,600 cc	Porsche 1600S	1st
	Sports Cars, unlimited	Porsche	1st (and ftd)
June 20			
Le Mans	24-Hour Race, Overall	Lotus Elite	10th
	Index of Performance		11th
	1,500 cc Class		2nd
July 5			
Zandvoort	World Cup Race	Lotus Elite	Ret.
July 11			
Bo'ness Hill Climb	Sports Cars, over 2,000 cc	Lister-Jaguar	1st (and ftd)
	Sports Cars, under 1,600 cc	Lotus Elite	1st
	Sports Cars, under 1,600 cc	Porsche 1600S	7th

Date and Circuit	Event	Car	Result
July 18			
Aintree	Sports Cars, over 2,000 cc	Lister-Jaguar	2nd
July 26			
Winfield Sprint	Sports Cars, over 1,500 cc	Lister-Jaguar	1st
	GT Cars, 1,000–2,000 cc	Lotus Elite	1st
	GT Cars, 1,000–2,000 cc	Porsche 1600S	2nd
	Formule Libre	Lister-Jaguar	1st (and ftd)
Aug. 2			
Mallory Park	Formule Libre, Heat	Lister-Jaguar	3rd
	Final	Lister-Jaguar	4th
	Sports Cars, over 1,200 cc, Heat	Lister-Jaguar	2nd
	Final	Lister-Jaguar	2nd
	GT Cars, up to 1,600 cc	Lotus Elite	2nd
Aug. 18			
Goodwood	Tourist Trophy	Tojeiro-Jaguar	Ret.

Date and Circuit	Event	Car	Result
Aug. 29			
Brands Hatch	World Cup Race,	Lotus	
	Heat 1	Elite	1st
	Heat 2	Lotus Elite	2nd
	Sports Cars, over 3,000 cc	Lister-Jaguar	1st
Sept. 13			
Mallory Park	Sports Cars, over 1,200 cc	Lister-Jaguar	1st
	Formule Libre, Heat	Lister-Jaguar	3rd
	Final	Lister-Jaguar	8th
	GT Cars, 1,000–1,600 cc	Lotus Elite	1st
Sept. 26			
Oulton Park	GT Cars, under 1,600 cc	Lotus Elite	1st
Sept. 27			
Charterhall	Sports Cars, over 1,500 cc	Lister-Jaguar	Ret.
	Sports Cars, under 1,300 cc	Lotus Elite	5th
	GT Cars, unlimited	Lotus Elite	1st

Date and Circuit	Event	Car	Result
Oct. 4			
Charterhall	Sports Cars, over 1,500 cc	Lister-Jaguar	1st
	Formule Libre	Lister-Jaguar	1st
	GT Cars, unlimited	Lotus Elite	1st
	Sports Cars, under 1,300 cc	Lotus Elite	4th
	BMRC Trophy Handicap	Lister-Jaguar	13th
Oct. 10			
Snetterton	Three Hours Race	Lotus Elite	1st
Dec. 26			
Brands Hatch	GT Cars, unlimited	Lotus Elite	Ret.
	Formula Junior	Gemini	Ret.

1960

Date and Circuit	Event	Car	Result
March 19			
Goodwood	Formula Junior	Lotus 18	1st
April 2			
Oulton Park	Formula Junior	Lotus 18	1st
	Sports Car Race	Aston Martin DBR1	3rd
April 10			
Brussels	Brussels Grand Prix (F2)	Lotus 18	Ret.

Date and Circuit	Event	Car	Result
April 16			
Goodwood	Formula Junior	Lotus 18	1st
	Sports Car Race	Aston Martin	Ret.
April 30			
Aintree	Aintree 200 (F2)	Lotus 18	Ret.
	Formula Junior	Lotus 18	Ret.
May 14			
Silverstone	Formula Junior	Lotus 18	1st
	Sports Car Race	Aston Martin	Ret.
May 22			
Nürburgring	1,000 Km	Aston Martin	Ret.
May 27			
Monaco	Formula Junior	Lotus 18	7th
June 5			
Zandvoort	Dutch Grand Prix	Lotus 18	Ret.
June 19			
Spa-Francorchamps	Belgian Grand Prix	Lotus 18	5th
June 25			
Le Mans	24-Hour Race	Aston Martin	3rd (overall)
July 3			
Rheims	French Grand Prix	Lotus 18	5th
July 16			
Silverstone	British Grand Prix	Lotus 18	16th

Date and Circuit	Event	Car	Result
July 24			
Solitude	South German Grand Prix (F2)	Lotus 18	8th
	Formula Junior	Lotus 18	1st
Aug. 1			
Brands Hatch	Guards Trophy Race (F1)	Lotus 18	Ret.
	Formula Junior	Lotus 18	1st
Aug. 14			
Oporto	Portuguese Grand Prix	Lotus 18	3rd
Aug. 19			
Goodwood	BARC FJ Championship	Lotus 18	2nd
Aug. 27			
Brands Hatch	Kentish Hundred (F2)	Lotus 18	1st
	Formula Junior	Lotus 18	2nd
Sept. 17			
Snetterton	Lombank Trophy (F1)	Lotus 18	2nd
	Formula Junior	Lotus 18	1st
Sept. 24			
Oulton Park	Gold Cup Race (F1)	Lotus 18	Ret.
	Formula Junior,		
	Heat 1	Lotus 18	1st
	Heat 2	Lotus 18	1st
Sept. 25			
Charterhall	Formule Libre	Lotus 18	Ret.
Nov. 20			
Riverside	United States Grand Prix	Lotus 18	16th

Date and Circuit	Event	Car	Result
Dec. 26			
Brands Hatch	John Davy Trophy (FJ)	Lotus 18	1st

1961

Date and Circuit	Event	Car	Result
Jan. 7			
Ardmore	New Zealand Grand Prix	Lotus 18	7th
Jan. 14			
Levin	Tasman Race	Lotus 18	2nd
Jan. 21			
Christchurch	Lady Wigram Trophy	Lotus 18	Ret.
April 3			
Pau	Pau Grand Prix	Lotus 18	1st
April 8			
Brussels	Brussels Grand Prix	Lotus 18	Ret.
April 22			
Aintree	Aintree 200	Lotus 18	8th
April 26			
Syracuse	Syracuse Grand Prix	Lotus 18	6th
May 6			
Silverstone	International Trophy (ICF)	Lotus 18	8th
May 14			
Monaco	Monaco Grand Prix	Lotus 21	10th

Date and Circuit	Event	Car	Result
May 21			
Zandvoort	Dutch Grand Prix	Lotus 21	3rd
May 28			
Nürburgring	1,000 Km	Aston Martin DBR1	Ret.
June 3			
Brands Hatch	Silver City Trophy	Lotus 21	2nd
June 9			
Le Mans	24-Hour Race	Aston Martin DBR1	Ret.
June 17			
Spa-Francorchamps	Belgian Grand Prix	Lotus 21	12th
July 3			
Rheims	French Grand Prix	Lotus 21	3rd
July 9			
Silverstone	British Empire Trophy (ICF)	Lotus 18	5th
July 15			
Aintree	British Grand Prix	Lotus 21	Ret.
July 23			
Solitude	South German Grand Prix	Lotus 21	7th
Aug. 6			
Nürburgring	German Grand Prix	Lotus 21	4th

Date and Circuit	Event	Car	Result
Aug. 7			
Brands Hatch	Guards Trophy (ICF)	Lotus 18	2nd
Aug. 19			
Goodwood	Tourist Trophy	Aston Martin DB4	4th
Aug. 20			
Karlskoga	Swedish Grand Prix	Lotus 21	Ret.
Aug. 27			
Roskildring	Danish Grand Prix (F1)	Lotus 18	Ret.
Sept. 3			
Modena	Modena Grand Prix	Lotus 21	4th
Sept. 10			
Monza	Italian Grand Prix	Lotus 21	Ret.
Sept. 17			
Zeltweg	Austrian Grand Prix	Lotus 21	4th
Sept. 23			
Oulton Park	Gold Cup	Lotus 21	Ret.
Sept. 24			
Charterhall	Formule Libre	Aston Martin DBR1	2nd
	Sports Cars, unlimited	Aston Martin DBR1	2nd

Date and Circuit	Event	Car	Result
Oct. 15 Montlhéry	Paris 1,000 Km	Aston Martin DB4	6th
Oct. 22 Watkins Glen	United States Grand Prix	Lotus 21	7th
Dec. 9 Kyalami	Rand Grand Prix	Lotus 21	1st
Dec. 17 Westmead	Natal Grand Prix	Lotus 21	1st
Dec. 26 East London	South African Grand Prix	Lotus 21	1st

1962

Date and Circuit	Event	Car	Result
Jan. 1 Cape Town	Cape Grand Prix	Lotus 21	2nd
Feb. 11 Daytona	Inter- Continental GT Race (1,300 cc class)	Lotus Elite	4th
March 12 Sandown	Formule Libre, Heat Final	Lotus 21 Lotus 21	2nd 6th

Date and Circuit	Event	Car	Result
April 1			
Brussels	Brussels Grand Prix	Lotus 24	Ret.
April 14			
Snetterton	Lombank Trophy	Lotus 24	1st
April 23			
Pau	Pau Grand Prix	Lotus 24	Ret.
April 28			
Aintree	Aintree 200	Lotus 24	1st
May 12			
Silverstone	International Trophy	Lotus 24	2nd
	Sports Car Race	Aston Martin	3rd
May 20			
Zandvoort	Dutch Grand Prix	Lotus 25	9th
May 27			
Nürburgring	1,000 Km	Lotus 23	Ret.
June 3			
Monaco	Monaco Grand Prix	Lotus 25	Ret.
June 11			
Mallory Park	2,000 Guineas	Lotus 25	Ret.
June 17			
Spa-Francorchamps	Belgian Grand Prix	Lotus 25	1st
July 1			
Rheims	Rheims Grand Prix	Lotus 25	Ret.

Date and Circuit	Event	Car	Result
July 8 Rouen	French Grand Prix	Lotus 25	Ret.
July 15 Solitude	South German Grand Prix	Lotus 25	Ret.
July 21 Aintree	British Grand Prix	Lotus 25	1st
Aug. 5 Nürburgring	German Grand Prix	Lotus 25	4th
Aug. 6 Brands Hatch	Guards Trophy	Lotus 23	Ret.
Aug. 18 Goodwood	Tourist Trophy	Aston Martin DB4	Ret.
Aug. 26 Ollon-Villars	Hill Climb	Lotus 21	3rd (class)
Sept. 1 Oulton Park	Sports Car Race Gold Cup	Lotus 23 Lotus 25	2nd 1st
Sept. 16 Monza	Italian Grand Prix	Lotus 25	Ret.
Sept. 29 Snetterton	Three Hours Race	Lotus 23	1st
Oct. 7 Watkins Glen	United States Grand Prix	Lotus 25	1st

Date and Circuit	Event	Car	Result
Oct. 21			
Montlhéry	Paris 1,000 Km	Aston Martin DB4	Ret.
Nov. 4			
Mexico City	Mexican Grand Prix	Lotus 25	1st
Dec. 15			
Kyalami	Rand Grand Prix	Lotus 25	1st
Dec. 22			
Westmead	Natal Grand Prix, Heat	Lotus 25	Ret.
	Final	Lotus 25	2nd
Dec. 29			
East London	South African Grand Prix	Lotus 25	Ret.

1963

March 30			
Snetterton	Lombank Trophy	Lotus 25	2nd
April 6			
Oulton Park	British Empire Trophy	Lotus 23	1st
April 15			
Pau	Pau Grand Prix	Lotus 25	1st
April 21			
Imola	Imola Grand Prix	Lotus 25	1st

Date and Circuit	Event	Car	Result
April 27			
Aintree	Aintree 200	Lotus 25	3rd
May 11			
Silverstone	International Trophy	Lotus 25	1st
May 26			
Monaco	Monaco Grand Prix	Lotus 25	Ret.
May 30			
Indianapolis	500-Mile Memorial Stakes	Lotus 29	2nd
June 1			
Mosport	Sports Car Race	Lotus 23	3rd (in class)
June 3			
Crystal Palace	Sports Car Race	Lotus 23	1st
June 9			
Spa-Francorchamps	Belgian Grand Prix	Lotus 25	1st
June 23			
Zandvoort	Dutch Grand Prix	Lotus 25	1st
June 30			
Rheims	French Grand Prix	Lotus 25	1st
July 20			
Silverstone	British Grand Prix	Lotus 25	1st
July 28			
Solitude	South German Grand Prix	Lotus 25	8th

Date and Circuit	Event	Car	Result
Aug. 4			
Nürburgring	German Grand Prix	Lotus 25	2nd
Aug. 5			
Brands Hatch	Saloon Car Race	Ford Galaxie	1st
Aug. 11			
Karlskoga	Swedish Grand Prix	Lotus 25	1st
Aug. 18			
Milwaukee	Milwaukee ' 200 '	Lotus 29	1st
Sept. 1			
Zeltweg	Austrian Grand Prix	Lotus 25	Ret.
Sept. 8			
Monza	Italian Grand Prix	Lotus 25	1st
Sept. 21			
Oulton Park	Gold Cup	Lotus 25	1st
	Sports Car Race	Lotus 23	1st
Sept. 22			
Trenton	State Fair Race	Lotus 29	Ret.
Sept. 28			
Snetterton	Three Hours Race	Lotus 23	1st
	Saloon Car Race	Lotus Cortina	1st
Oct. 6			
Watkins Glen	United States Grand Prix	Lotus 25	3rd

Date and Circuit	Event	Car	Result
Oct. 13 Riverside	Riverside Grand Prix	Lotus 23B	1st
Oct. 20 Laguna Seca	Monterey Grand Prix	Lotus 19	Ret.
Oct. 27 Mexico City	Mexican Grand Prix	Lotus 25	1st
Dec. 14 Kyalami	Rand Grand Prix	Lotus 25	Ret.
Dec. 28 East London	South African Grand Prix	Lotus 25	1st

1964

Date and Circuit	Event	Car	Result
March 14 Snetterton	*Daily Mirror* Trophy	Lotus 25	Ret.
	Saloon Car Race	Lotus Cortina	2nd (1st in class)
March 22 Sebring	Saloon Car Race	Lotus Cortina	3rd (1st in class)
March 23 Sebring	12 Hours	Lotus Cortina	21st (2nd in class)

Date and Circuit	Event	Car	Result
March 30			
Goodwood	International Trophy	Lotus 25	1st
	Saloon Car Race	Lotus Cortina	2nd (1st in class)
April 5			
Pau	Pau Grand Prix (F2)	Lotus 32	1st
April 11			
Oulton Park	Saloon Car Race	Lotus Cortina	1st
	G.T. Race	Lotus Elan	1st
	Sports Car Race	Lotus 19	1st
April 18			
Aintree	Aintree 200	Lotus 25	Ret.
	Sports Car Race	Lotus 30	2nd
	Saloon Car Race	Lotus Cortina	3rd
April 26			
Nürburgring	Eifelrennen (F2)	Lotus 32	1st
May 2			
Silverstone	International Trophy	Lotus 25	Ret.
	Sports Car Race	Lotus 30	Ret.
	Saloon Car Race	Lotus Cortina	3rd (1st in class)
	G.T. Race	Lotus Elan	1st (in class)

Date and Circuit	Event	Car	Result
May 10			
Monaco	Monaco Grand Prix	Lotus 25	4th
May 16			
Mallory Park	Grovewood Trophy (F2)	Lotus 25	1st
	Guards Trophy	Lotus 30	1st
May 18			
Crystal Palace	London Trophy (F2), Heat Final	Lotus 25	2nd 10th
	Saloon Car Race	Lotus Cortina	1st
May 24			
Zandvoort	Dutch Grand Prix	Lotus 25	1st
May 30			
Indianapolis	500 Mile Memorial Stakes	Lotus 34	Ret.
June 14			
Spa-Francorchamps	Belgian Grand Prix	Lotus 25	1st
June 28			
Rouen	French Grand Prix	Lotus 25	Ret.
July 5			
Rheims	Rheims Grand Prix (F2)	Lotus 32	4th
July 11			
Brands Hatch	British Grand Prix	Lotus 25	1st

Date and Circuit	Event	Car	Result
July 19			
Solitude	South German Grand Prix	Lotus 25	1st
Aug. 2			
Nürburgring	German Grand Prix	Lotus 33	Ret.
Aug. 3			
Brands Hatch	British Eagle Trophy (F2)	Lotus 32	1st
	Guards Trophy	Lotus 30	Ret.
	Saloon Car Race	Lotus Cortina	2nd (1st in class)
Aug. 9			
Karlskoga	Canon Race (F2)	Lotus 32	2nd
Aug. 16			
Enna	Mediterranean Grand Prix	Lotus 33	2nd
Aug. 23			
Zeltweg	Austrian Grand Prix	Lotus 33	Ret.
Aug. 29			
Goodwood	Tourist Trophy	Lotus 30	12th
Sept. 6			
Monza	Italian Grand Prix	Lotus 33	Ret.
Sept. 13			
Albi	Albi Grand Prix (F2)	Lotus 32	Ret.

Date and Circuit	Event	Car	Result
Sept. 19 Oulton Park	Gold Cup (F2) Saloon Car Race	Lotus 32 Lotus Cortina	2nd 1st
Sept. 26 Mosport	Sports Car Race	Lotus 30	Ret.
Sept. 27 Trenton	USAC Race	Lotus 34	Ret.
Oct. 4 Watkins Glen	United States Grand Prix	Lotus 33	Ret.
Oct. 11 Riverside	*Times* Grand Prix	Lotus 30	3rd
Oct. 25 Mexico City	Mexican Grand Prix	Lotus 33	Ret.

1965

Date and Circuit	Event	Car	Result
Jan. 1 East London	South African Grand Prix	Lotus 33	1st
Jan. 10 Ardmore	New Zealand Grand Prix, Heat Final	Lotus 32	1st Ret.

Date and Circuit	Event	Car	Result
Jan. 16			
Levin	Tasman Cup, Race		
	Heat	Lotus 32	1st
	Final		1st
	' Flying Farewell '	Lotus 32	1st
Jan. 23			
Christchurch	Lady Wigram Trophy, Heat	Lotus 32	1st
	Final		1st
Jan. 30			
Invercargill	Teretonga Trophy, Heat	Lotus 32	1st
	Final		1st
	' Flying Farewell '	Lotus 32	2nd
Feb. 14			
Warwick Farm	Tasman Cup	Lotus 32	1st
Feb. 21			
Sandown Park	Tasman Cup	Lotus 32	2nd
March 1			
Longford	Tasman Cup		
	Heat	Lotus 32	5th
	Final		5th
March 7			
Lakeside	Tasman Cup	Lotus 32	1st

Date and Circuit	Event	Car	Result
March 13 Brands Hatch	Race of Champions, Heat Final	Lotus 33	1st Ret.
	Saloon Car Race	Lotus Cortina	Ret.
March 20 Silverstone	Guards Trophy	Lotus 30	1st
March 26 Sebring	Three Hours Race	Lotus Cortina	1st
April 4 Syracuse	Syracuse Grand Prix	Lotus 33	1st
April 10 Snetterton	Formula 2, Heat 1 Heat 2 Overall	Lotus 32	2nd 5th 3rd
	Saloon Car Race	Lotus Cortina	2nd (class)
April 19 Goodwood	International Trophy	Lotus 33	1st
	Sports Car Race	Lotus 30	1st
	Saloon Car Race	Lotus Cortina	1st
April 25 Pau	Pau Grand Prix (F2)	Lotus 32	1st

Date and Circuit	Event	Car	Result
May 1			
Oulton Park	Tourist Trophy	Lotus 30	Ret.
May 31			
Indianapolis	500-Mile Memorial Stakes	Lotus 38	1st
June 5			
Mosport	Sports Car Race	Lotus 30	Ret.
June 7			
Crystal Palace	London Trophy (F2), Heat 1	Lotus 32	1st
	Heat 2		1st
	Overall		1st
June 13			
Spa-Francorchamps	Belgian Grand Prix	Lotus 33	1st
June 27			
Clermont-Ferrand	French Grand Prix	Lotus 25	1st
July 3			
Rheims	Rheims Grand Prix (F2)	Lotus 35	3rd
July 10			
Silverstone	British Grand Prix	Lotus 33	1st
July 18			
Zandvoort	Dutch Grand Prix	Lotus 33	1st
Aug. 1			
Nürburgring	German Grand Prix	Lotus 33	1st

Date and Circuit	Event	Car	Result
Aug. 15			
Enna	Mediterranean Grand Prix	Lotus 35	2nd
Aug. 30			
Brands Hatch	British Eagle Trophy (F2)	Lotus 35	1st
	Sports Car Race, Heat 1	Lotus 40	8th
	Heat 2		Ret.
	Saloon Car Race	Lotus Cortina	Ret.
Sept. 12			
Monza	Italian Grand Prix	Lotus 33	Ret.
Sept. 18			
Oulton Park	Gold Cup (F2)	Lotus 35	6th
	Saloon Car Race	Lotus Cortina	2nd
Oct. 3			
Watkins Glen	United States Grand Prix	Lotus 33	Ret.
Oct. 24			
Mexico City	Mexican Grand Prix	Lotus 33	Ret.

1966

Jan. 8			
Pukekohe	New Zealand Grand Prix	Lotus 39	Ret.
Jan. 15			
Levin	Gold Leaf Trophy	Lotus 39	2nd

Date and Circuit	Event	Car	Result
Jan. 22			
Christchurch	Lady Wigram Trophy	Lotus 39	Ret.
Jan. 29			
Invercargill	Teretonga Trophy	Lotus 39	Ret.
Feb. 13			
Warwick Farm	Tasman Cup Race	Lotus 39	1st
Feb. 20			
Lakeside	Australian Grand Prix	Lotus 39	3rd
Feb. 27			
Sandown Park	Tasman Cup Race	Lotus 39	2nd
March 6			
Longford	Tasman Cup Race	Lotus 39	7th
April 8			
Snetterton	Saloon Car Race	Lotus Cortina	3rd (1st in class)
April 11			
Goodwood	International Trophy (F2)	Lotus 35	Ret.
	Saloon Car Race	Lotus Cortina	4th (1st in class)
April 17			
Pau	Pau Grand Prix (F2)	Lotus 35	7th
April 24			
Barcelona	Juan Jover (F2)	Lotus 44	Ret.

Date and Circuit	Event	Car	Result
May 22 Monaco	Monaco Grand Prix	Lotus 33	Ret.
May 30 Indianapolis	500-Mile Memorial Stakes	Lotus 38	2nd
June 13 Spa- Francorchamps	Belgian Grand Prix	Lotus 33	Ret.
July 16 Brands Hatch	British Grand Prix	Lotus 33	4th
July 24 Zandvoort	Dutch Grand Prix	Lotus 33	3rd
Aug. 7 Nürburgring	German Grand Prix	Lotus 33	Ret.
Aug. 21 Karlskoga	Formula 2 Race	Lotus 44	3rd
Aug. 28 Keimola	Formula 2 Race	Lotus 44	3rd
Aug. 29 Brands Hatch	Guards Trophy, Heat 1	Felday 4	1st (in class)
	Heat 2		Ret.
	Saloon Car Race	Lotus Cortina	1st

Date and Circuit	Event	Car	Result
Sept. 4			
Monza	Italian Grand Prix	Lotus 43	Ret.
Sept. 17			
Oulton Park	Gold Cup	Lotus 33	3rd
	Saloon Car Race	Lotus Cortina	1st.
Oct. 2			
Watkins Glen	United States Grand Prix	Lotus 43	1st
Oct. 23			
Mexico City	Mexican Grand Prix	Lotus 43	Ret.
Oct. 30			
Brands Hatch	Motor Show 200 (F2), Heat	Lotus 44	3rd
	Final		3rd
Nov. 19 *et seq*			
—	R.A.C. Rally	Lotus Cortina	Ret.

1967

Date and Circuit	Event	Car	Result
Jan. 7			
Pukekohe	New Zealand Grand Prix	Lotus 33	2nd
Jan. 14			
Levin	Tasman Cup	Lotus 33	1st
Jan. 21			
Christchurch	Lady Wigram Trophy	Lotus 33	1st

Date and Circuit	Event	Car	Result
Jan. 28			
Invercargill	Teretonga Trophy	Lotus 33	1st
Feb. 12			
Lakeside	Tasman Cup Race	Lotus 33	1st
Feb. 19			
Warwick Farm	Australian Grand Prix	Lotus 33	2nd
Feb. 26			
Sandown Park	Tasman Cup Race	Lotus 33	1st
March 6			
Longford	Tasman Cup Race	Lotus 33	2nd
April 2			
Pau	Pau Grand Prix (F2)	Lotus 48	4th
April 9			
Barcelona	Formula 2 Race	Lotus 48	1st
April 23			
Nürburgring (South Circuit)	Eifelrennen (F2)	Lotus 48	Ret.
May 7			
Monaco	Monaco Grand Prix	Lotus 33	Ret.
May 21			
Zolder	Formula 2, Heat 1	Lotus 48	1st
	Heat 2		4th
	Overall		Ret.
May 30–31			
Indianapolis	500-Mile Memorial Stakes	Lotus 38	Ret.

Date and Circuit	Event	Car	Result
June 4			
Zandvoort	Dutch Grand Prix	Lotus 49	1st
June 18			
Spa-Francorchamps	Belgian Grand Prix	Lotus 49	6th
June 25			
Rheims	Rheims Grand Prix (F2)	Lotus 48	Ret.
July 2			
Le Mans	French Grand Prix	Lotus 49	Ret.
July 9			
Rouen	Formula 2 Race	Lotus 48	Ret.
July 15			
Silverstone	British Grand Prix	Lotus 49	1st
July 16			
Tulln-Langenlebarn	Formula 2 Race	Lotus 48	Ret.
July 23			
Jarama	Formula 2 Race	Lotus 48	1st
Aug. 6			
Nürburgring	German Grand Prix	Lotus 49	Ret.
Aug. 27			
Mosport	Canadian Grand Prix	Lotus 49	Ret.
Aug. 13			
Karlskoga	Formula 2 Race	Lotus 48	3rd

Date and Circuit	Event	Car	Result
Sept. 3			
Keimola	Formula 2	Lotus 48	1st
Sept. 5			
Hameenlinna	Formula 2	Lotus 48	3rd
Sept. 10			
Monza	Italian Grand Prix	Lotus 49	3rd
Sept. 24			
Albi	Formula 2	Lotus 48	3rd
Oct. 1			
Watkins Glen	United States Grand Prix	Lotus 49	1st
Oct. 22			
Mexico City	Mexican	Lotus 49	1st
Oct. 29			
Rockingham	Rockingham 500 (stock cars)	Ford Fairlane	Ret.
Nov. 5			
Riverside	Rex Mays 300	Vollstedt-Ford	Ret.
Nov. 12			
Jarama	Spanish Grand Prix	Lotus 49	1st

1968

Date and Circuit	Event	Car	Result
Jan. 1			
Kyalami	South African Grand Prix	Lotus 49	1st
Jan. 6			
Pukekohe	New Zealand Grand Prix	Lotus 49	Ret.

Date and Circuit	Event	Car	Result
Jan. 13			
Levin	Tasman Cup Race	Lotus 49	Ret.
Jan. 20			
Christchurch	Lady Wigram Trophy	Lotus 49	1st
Jan. 28			
Invercargill	Teretonga Trophy	Lotus 49	2nd
Feb. 11			
Surfers Paradise	Tasman Cup Race	Lotus 49	1st
Feb. 18			
Warwick Farm	Tasman Cup Race	Lotus 49	1st
Feb. 25			
Sandown Park	Australian Grand Prix	Lotus 49	1st
March 4			
Longford	Tasman Cup Race	Lotus 49	5th
March 31			
Barcelona	Formula 2 Race	Lotus 48	Ret.
April 7			
Hockenheim . .			